Rory Ross has been a journalist since graduating from Cambridge where he read history. He is now a freelance contributor to publications such as *Tatler* and the *Daily Telegraph*. He rowed against Steve Redgrave at Marlow Regatta in 1979 – and lost.

Tim Foster is one of Britain's most technically gifted oarsmen, the first to win two successive World Junior Championship gold medals. He is now chief coach at University of London Boat Club, apprentice coach for the British Olympic rowing team and a broadcaster at the BBC.

FOUR MEN IN A BOAT

THE INSIDE STORY OF THE SYDNEY 2000 COXLESS FOUR

Rory Ross, with Tim Foster

PHOENIX

A PHOENIX PAPERBACK

First published in Great Britain in 2004
by Weidenfeld & Nicolson
This paperback edition published in 2005
by Phoenix
an imprint of Orion Books Ltd,
Orion House, 5 Upper St Martin's Lane,
London, WC2H 9EA

10 9 8 7 6 5 4 3 2 1

A CIP catalogue record for this book
is available from the British Library.

ISBN 0 75381 883 3

Typeset by Selwood Systems, Midsomer Norton

Printed and bound in Great Britain by

www.orionbooks.co.uk

To: Sarah, Isabella, Alexander, Emily. RR
To: James, Steve, Matthew, Jürgen, Mum, Dad and Jason. TF

Contents

List of Illustrations

The crew loosening up © *Shaun Botterill, courtesy of Allsports*
The crew's debut in April 1997 © *John Shore*
Steve Redgrave announces his comeback © *John Shore*
Prize-giving at Henley Royal Regatta, 1997 © *John Shore*
The final of the Stewards' Challenge Cup in 1998 © *John Shore*
Jürgen Grobler, *courtesy Peter Spurrier/Intersport-Images*
Tim Foster © *John Shore*
Training in Seville, *courtesy of Allsports*
The Stewards' Challenge Cup, Henley, 2000 © *John Shore*
Steve, Matthew and Tim © *John Shore*
Atlanta Olympics 1996, *courtesy Tim Foster*
Sydney 2000, *courtesy Tim Foster*
Tim Foster with his father, *courtesy Tim Foster*
BBC Sports Personality of the Year © *John Shore*
Sydney 2000, the final, *courtesy Peter Spurrier/Intersport-Images*
The crew's final journey © *John Shore*

Every effort has been made to contact holders of material quoted and reproduced in this book, but any omissions will be restituted at the earliest opportunity.

1

The Big Chat

Friday, 22 September 2000

It was the eve of the final of the coxless fours at the Sydney Olympics. The British crew of Steve Redgrave, Matthew Pinsent, James Cracknell and Tim Foster were due to meet their coach Jürgen Grobler at 6 p.m. Their mood that day had been light-hearted. They'd spent the morning at Penrith rowing lake outside Sydney, had returned to Sydney for lunch, a rest and a stretch, and had been soaking up the atmosphere of the Olympic Village, lolling about on a grass square, surrounded by tracksuited athletes colourfully and purposefully running, jogging, stretching and going through drills of motion. As they filed into Grobler's small apartment – Foster taking care to remove the blade of grass on which he'd been philosophically chewing – the crew felt the tension begin to mount.

Grobler, 52, chief coach of the British Olympic rowing team, was in sole charge of the British four. His small, functional flat was mercifully located in a different block from the oarsmen, for he snored 'like a trooper.' It boasted a kitchen and 'lounge'. The fastidiously made bed, flawlessly piled papers, neatly arranged laptop and printer, and conspicuous absence of strewn clothing bore the stamp of Grobler's personality.

Wherever in the world he travelled as Britain's chief rowing coach, he kept his rooms and possessions in immaculate order – so unlike James Cracknell.

Since arriving in England in 1991, Grobler had successfully adapted to the British way of life in many ways; but occasionally his East German roots would show. The East German hour, for example, contained fifty-five minutes. If Grobler said, 'Meet at six,' he'd ring you at three minutes to six with, 'Vhere are you?'

So at five minutes to six the crew assembled in Grobler's rigidly straightened apartment. They sat seance-like in a circle, like four massive pillars, dressed in crested navy Great Britain sweatshirts in preference to the garish and shiny Great Britain tracksuit. A sick nervousness hummed inside them as they consulted each other with eyes only.

The Olympics are so much more than just a rowing race, thought Foster, as he glanced outside at the busy grass square where a few minutes earlier the crew had been stretching and warming up, under the shadow of the Olympic stadium. *It's about theatre, fellowship, the Village, the focused attention and the whole circus.*

Grobler took the floor. Straight to the point, man to man, eyeball to eyeball, he spoke. 'Chames,' he said, fixing Cracknell and pressing 'play'. 'You are the most powerful bowman in the world. You are so strong, no one can beat you.'

He turned to Redgrave and Pinsent. 'Steve, Matthew, you are Olympic champions and world-beaters. No one will beat you when you put on the power . . .'

Grobler's fists pumped the air and his face reddened. Foster and Cracknell subconsciously followed him, and pumped the air too. 'Tim? . . .' There was a pause. At 86 kilograms and 6 feet 3 inches tall, Foster was the 'smallest' and 'weakest' of the crew. Grobler picked his words carefully. '. . . Tim, you row very well . . .'

Grobler was as keyed up as anyone. His accent and barely suppressed emotions lent his words power. Although familiar in pattern, Grobler's 'pre-race' was one of his strengths. Even during the early 1990s, when his English wasn't so good, his pre-race had hit the spot; and he never shied from the agony of rowing. '... The man with the hammer will come,' he said, burning the crew up with his eyes. 'He'll be waiting for you. It will be tough. It will be bloody tough ...' Grobler's accent was another East German import. His voice resonated up from his stomach in guttural Teutonic growls. Whenever he got excited, he sounded like a bear trying to chew a wasp. This bear was trying to work through the whole nest.

Grobler then delivered his traditional, ringing, burn-your-bridges trumpet call. He talked about the next day's race, about how no other crew could live with them, and about how confident they should be of victory. Tactics never changed: go off hard, get ahead, dictate the race. Whatever else happened in rowing, Grobler could be relied upon to talk confidence, power, leading from the start and rowing your own race. Had he come up with something new, like, 'The Italians will be strong,' he'd have thrown the crew into panic.

On paper, the British four had much to be confident about. Anointed World Champions the previous three years, they had won the Steward's Challenge Cup at Henley Royal Regatta (for international-standard coxless fours) four times, and the World Cup yellow jersey (competed for at international regattas in Europe each summer) three times. The sole blot on their record was their last competitive foray at Lucerne International Regatta two months earlier, when they had been defeated by one tenth of a second in their semi-final and by a whopping eight seconds in their final – a disastrous performance but one from which the crew had learnt much during the intervening two months.

Redgrave took the floor. He leaned forwards, looked down

and recapped the race plan. 'We'll go off at 46 to 47 strokes a minute. After 15 strokes, I'll call "stride". The rate will come down to 42 to 43. We'll approach the first minute rating 40. I'll then call another "stride". The rate will come down to 37, we'll lengthen out and settle into a race pace. If anyone tries to keep up with us, it'll cost them.'

It wasn't Henry V at Agincourt – Redgrave was too impassive for that. Without eyeing any individual, he merely stated, most matter-of-factly, what would happen: the start, the rhythm, the pace, the push. He could have been commentating on a football match about which he couldn't have cared less, or describing the goal of the century in terms of 'A passes to B, who passes to C, who dribbles past four players, shoots and scores.' He never spoke about winning a historic fifth Olympic gold medal for himself. Never in the preceding four years had he once mentioned it to the crew. His previous four Olympic gold medals were very literally in the past, filling their own display case in the Rowing and River Museum at Henley-on-Thames.

Redgrave's words whipped at Cracknell's blood; the crew sensed him twitching. Perhaps they failed to strike the same chord in Foster. They were more what he wanted to hear from Redgrave, because he'd heard them many times before during the three-and-a-half-year odyssey since the four had been launched at the Leander Club at Henley in April 1997. Had Redgrave said, 'Let's go out and give it a go' – now that would have been a shock.

Then the mood changed. Redgrave became more expressive. Without actually standing on the table and hoisting the flag, he talked about how Olympic titles were for life, not just one year. He recalled his previous Olympic wins and how good they'd felt. He spoke about how confident he was that the crew would win. While Foster stared at a dot he'd found on the table in front of him, Cracknell by now had ants in his pants. For the first time in months, he had found himself with unaccustomed energy in his nerves and time on his hands, as happens to athletes as their training tapers before their Big Day. He was shifting restlessly and growing jittery.

Pep talks ordinarily ended with Redgrave's speech and 'Any questions?' Unusually, Pinsent took the floor. He briefly added to Redgrave's words, applying his own spin. He mentioned losing at Lucerne, but said that the crew had leapt ahead since then. He talked about their abilities, how he wanted the race to go, and how the outcome was in their hands. Without causing anyone to break out in a nervous sweat, Pinsent caught the spirit of the occasion.

It was Foster's turn. Four years earlier, rowing in the same boat at the Atlanta Olympics, Foster had found himself in almost exactly the same situation. 'We'd performed poorly at Lucerne,' he said, 'then returned to form just before Atlanta, did well in the heats and semi-final, and were favourites for gold. Four and a half minutes into the final, all six crews were level; but our race didn't go to plan: we finished third in the toughest race of my career. We lost gold by 0.91 of a second. It has taken me four years to reach the same point again. But I don't want the same result . . .' Foster felt the emotion of the moment begin to overwhelm him. What he wanted to put into words felt so colossal that he couldn't articulate it in the way he wanted. Had he let it all splurge out, he felt he'd have gone to pieces or turned into a quivering blancmange.

This was the most intensely felt moment of the crew's existence. Not even Cracknell and Foster's late-night analyses strayed so deep into emotional territory. For the crew to address the question *Why?* was new. Normally *What?* sufficed.

Four pairs of eyes, including Grobler's, bored into Cracknell. James was fighting a low-emotional-threshold panic. His nerves were like overtuned E-strings. Even more verbally constipated and emotionally charged than Foster, he fought back tears as he mumbled a few words about how inspiring it was to row with three such motivated athletes. Cracknell's crew-mates had each felt that they'd had something to say; Cracknell felt he'd had something to receive. He was ready to race there and then – or break down.

The psychology of the crew changed perceptibly. Bonds of steel forged during the previous three and a half years drew that little bit tighter. They'd all felt it, but no one had mentioned it. Each crew member had approached the task of winning Olympic gold in his own way. This much was clear from the previous four years' training. Their respective gifts, talents and abilities had been exhaustively measured and assessed, and the results shared out. They'd duelled in boats, in gyms, on cycling sorties and on ergometer machines which simulate the rowing stroke. They'd lived together, eaten together and room-shared for hundreds of days. Grobler had tested their endurance, power, physiology, psychology and technique. They knew each other's strengths, weaknesses and flaws better than their own brothers' and sisters'. What had been missing?

'After that meeting, I felt for the first time that we were "in the same boat",' says Foster. 'We were ready to race. I've always thought it was a good sign when I want a race to happen *now!* Had you asked me one week earlier, "Are you ready?" I would have said, "No! One more week!" But from that moment, I no longer dreaded the final. I wanted it to happen.'

The meeting finished with fourteen hours to go before the race. The crew split up. Pinsent returned to his room and the mini-library of books that he carried around with him; he ate little food before a race, but devoured books. Cracknell, unable to eat or sleep, wandered to the British Olympic Association headquarters located in the utility room of the garage of a three-storey block of flats in the Village. A large screen was showing a live television feed from the BBC in London. *Good to take your mind off things by watching television*, he thought, as he settled down. Redgrave and Foster found themselves with time to kill, feeling hungry and only three minutes' walk from the Olympic food tent. The two oarsmen made their final visit to the 'healthy-eating' section with its pasta and fibrous glossy vegetables, fruit and rice. Foster said goodbye to the fibrous glossy staff whom he'd befriended during the previous fortnight. He dribbled at the glutinous thought of the mission-accomplished, unbuttoned-with-relief week that lay ahead after tomorrow's race. No way was he going near that rabbit food again, he thought, as his mind idled towards the curries, fries and burgers.

As Redgrave and Foster unwound from Grobler's call to arms, they switched to silly-joke mode; and what better material for silly jokes than the Olympic food tent, a freak-show of physiological extremes? Some athletes, especially the basketball players, towered over seven feet tall; others, squat, thigh-chafing Near Eastern weightlifters, seemed at least seven feet wide. Redgrave and Foster played 'guess the sport'. Steve, at 6 feet 4 inches, deliberately queued behind the Russian basketball team to see how high he came up against them. They towered head and shoulders above him. It was an amusing if distracting place. They touched on the race, laughed about Cracknell and wondered what he'd be up to.

Settling down in the British Olympic headquarters, Cracknell looked forward to watching *Grandstand*, the BBC's flagship sports programme. After the opening sequence, Steve Rider, the *Grandstand* anchorman, greeted viewers with, 'Good evening. Only thirteen and a half hours to go before the start of the coxless fours final.'

'Aaargh! Just what I didn't need!' yelled Cracknell, leaping up, totally psyched, and fleeing back to his room.

Later, Foster found him a gibbering wreck, pacing up and down, no way ready for sleep, checking and rechecking his bag for his dark glasses, up on his bed, down on the floor again, wearing a hole in the carpet, like a hamster on speed. 'I know, I know,' he said; 'it's pathetic.'

Cracknell knew he was an emotional time bomb. He'd over-train, push himself to breaking point, topple over the edge, fall ill and need time off. His CV came with a doctor's note. Before Atlanta, a potential finalist in the double scull with Bobby Thatcher (son of Russ Thatcher, boatman to the Great Britain rowing team), he'd overtrained and gone down with tonsillitis on the day of the opening ceremony. At Sydney he was more in control, but only just.

While Cracknell thrashed about in his upper bunk bed, Foster slept like a baby, which one shouldn't. Not before a big race. One should be on edge. 'I'd not been looking forward to that night's sleep for four years,' says Foster. 'But not to recall anything of it was unusual. One should be nervous. Nerves are your friends. Nerves should be encouraged.'

4 a.m. Saturday, 23 September 2000

Filled with positive anticipation, not mental dread, Foster rose forty-five minutes earlier than the rest of the crew. He woke Mark Edgar, the rowing team's chief physiotherapist. Together they went through their stretching routine to a somnolent athletes' chorus of snores, laboured breathing and grunts. Foster sat on the physio bed, feet sticking out over the edge. Edgar placed one of Foster's legs on his shoulder, while pinning his other leg down on the table. Then Edgar slowly levered Foster's leg upwards. After the appropriate *plink! plank! plunk!* twanging of hamstrings was heard, he repeated the exercise on the other leg. Edgar then massaged Foster's back.

I've come this far, thought Foster, as Edgar palpated and

pummelled away. *Nothing will stop me now. I want to think about the race – and row the race – without worrying about anything.*

The stretching lasted one hour. By now the others were up. As they left for breakfast, Foster's lack of nerves surprised him. He reviewed the crew's build-up with confidence, even self-satisfaction. He took heart from his crew-mates' optimism. *It's in our hands*, he thought. *Jürgen, Matthew, James and Steve will do their bit, and more than their bit.*

Heartily, he tucked into yoghurt, fruit, cereal and toast. 'It's all right for some,' mumbled Pinsent. Grobler said little. After breakfast the crew went directly by minibus to the rowing course at Penrith outside Sydney.

Comically bulging out of their seats, knees behind their ears, they travelled in silence, Dr Ann Redgrave, Steve's wife, at the wheel. Cracknell sat, eyes shut, headset on. Pinsent dozed in his usual front seat. Arriving at a dark, chilly Penrith, the crew made their way to the British tent, near where their boat rested on a rack in one of the boat tents. Foster found a patch of concrete and stretched his back for twenty-five minutes. Redgrave and Cracknell warmed up on rowing machines. Pinsent, who rarely put in more physical effort than was absolutely necessary, and who seemed to regard the whole process of warming up as in some way effete or underhand, didn't bother.

7 a.m.

Three and a half hours remained until the biggest moment of their lives so far. Grobler checked the nuts and bolts that fastened the riggers on to the side of the boat. He measured the spans of the riggers and the oars to check that none of them had inexplicably altered overnight.

Although boat tents are locked overnight, it is a matter

of trust that one doesn't nobble or accidentally-on-purpose damage one's opponents' kit. That wouldn't be cricket. There had been a rumoured nobbling a few years earlier when someone had crept into the boat tent at night and changed the gearing on a set of blades. 'Gearing' here refers to the ratio between the inboard and outboard lengths of the oar. A highly geared crew will start a race at a blistering pace, but will often flag in the latter stages. A lowly geared crew will start slower, but find it easier to sustain the pace. More common than actual nobbling, as Grobler himself could have told you, was to measure your opposition's gearing for a clue as to possible race tactics.

As Grobler busily scurried around the boat with his short, purposeful gait, you could tell he was nervous by how tight he'd fastened the 10 millimetre nuts on the riggers. Either he'd given them one big yank or had repeatedly tweaked them. No crew had a cleaner boat that day. Grobler, never above dirtying his hands, had cleaned, polished and buffed the boat to a dazzling sheen.

It was time for a pre-race paddle: 4 kilometres, one length of the lake and back. As the sun peeped over the horizon and lit up breathless Penrith, the crew paddled up the warm-up loop, which joined the main 2000 metre course at the Finish and at a point 750 metres from the Start. They continued up to the Start, turned around, and paddled back down again. As the blades chopped into the water and levered the boat forward, then exited the water, the boat made a noise like *tch-aaaaaargh-tch-aaaaaaargh-tch-aaaaaargh* ... The crew's bulk, rendered in mists, gilded by the orange sun, made such a spectacle that someone photographed the four and published the picture as a postcard.

Redgrave called for two 'heart-starter' bursts of 15 strokes at 'hard pressure', one at 24 strokes per minute, the other at 28. As the crew crossed the finishing line, their thoughts shooting in all directions, the *tch-aaaaaargh-tch-aaaaaaargh-tch-aaaaaargh* was interrupted by wild cheers from a group of about a hundred early-rising British fans. Among them was a chap from Birmingham who, after Atlanta, had decided to save up and travel to watch Pinsent – and, as it proved, Redgrave too – race at Sydney in 2000. At 5 a.m. he had taken his seat at the finishing line and draped a Union flag over the side of the grandstand. The flag and the cheering boosted the crew's heart rate far more than the 15 stroke bursts. 'If there's one thing madder than a rower,' thought Foster, 'it's a rowing fan.'

The paddle felt comfortable. The power was never in doubt. It was a question of applying it. Twitchy at low pressures, the boat tended to lurch from side to side; but the crew could easily convince themselves that that was their best paddle ever. If the boat lurched and wobbled, it lurched and wobbled *consistently – balletically*. Hearts pounding, they paddled to the landing stage. They'd each felt the buzz and sensed that their crew-mates had felt it too.

After the outing, the crew briefly chatted. 'I joked that the paddling was really good,' says Foster. 'Someone replied, "You always say that." I actually thought it *was* good. Before the Games, we ironed out a lot of technical wrinkles, like emphasising the front end of the stroke, the catch and the connection, and putting the "power peak" earlier in the stroke. Everything had come together.'

'OK, are you ready?' asked Grobler, omitting the usual post-outing analysis. The crew then went into their own pre-race rituals while Jürgen all but disappeared.

They lay down and rested. As a crew, you learn to appreciate when to talk to your mates, and when to leave them alone. This was the time to avoid Cracknell and Pinsent. Lost in his own world, Cracknell, Walkman clamped on, exuded a 'don't talk to me' air. Pinsent sat quietly in a corner with a book. Redgrave wandered about. Contrary to the rowing textbook, which says that the body's pre-race adrenaline should keep you on edge, Foster overdid the relaxation and accidentally drifted off for twenty minutes.

The crew could hear the commentaries on races due off before theirs. Where they had predicted clear outcomes, the races were proving real gut-busters with blanket finishes. Each member of the four faced the nerve-jangling, blood-stirring experience of a big race in different ways.

'When the pressure is at its most mild,' said Pinsent, 'we talk about "going twitchy". You can't sit still. Anyone who didn't know you would think you were hyperactive. The next step up involves lethargy, a complete loss of appetite. After that you begin to convince yourself that you're ill. You feel nauseous. You worry because you have a dry throat or a bad headache. You tell yourself your arm is hurting badly.'

Waiting for his first heat in the pairs at the Atlanta Olympics, Pinsent's body had effectively been hijacked by nerves. 'I was lying there in the crew tent taking a drink,' he said. 'I was feeling nervous, but in control. Suddenly, I thought, "Hang on, I'm going to chuck up here." I pulled the wall of the marquee back, yakked up my bottle of Powerade, and lay back down again. I thought to myself, "Well, there's no going back. Call a doctor now and he'll only give you a right slap and tell you to get on with it." So I did. After a while you realise everyone is feeling the same.'

Redgrave was not a man to do more talking than the exigencies of communication required, and was best avoided before a race. He became tetchy and difficult, and often talked to himself. At Atlanta the pressure had told. Transport problems and a health scare among the British rowing team had piled on the stress. Lacklustre British performances had thrown a spotlight on to Redgrave's vow, made after winning at Barcelona, that he'd strike gold again at Atlanta; but the logistical mayhem of Atlanta had wound him up no end. He was a pain to have around. Black was white, and white was black. He was a big kid in a foul mood. One particular Redgrave moment stuck in the memory. Two days before the final of the coxless pairs at Atlanta, some post for Redgrave had been misdirected to the coxless four of Tim Foster, Rupert Obholzer and Jonny and Greg Searle. That afternoon, after training, Jonny Searle went to Redgrave and said, 'Here's your post.'

'About time too,' grunted Redgrave.

'Hang on,' answered Searle, 'I'm not your postman. Why is it my job to find you to give you your post?'

Silence fell on the squad as Redgrave at 105 kilograms squared up to Searle at 89. Pinsent and Foster cut each other anxious glances.

After what seemed several minutes, Searle said to Redgrave, 'Do you have a problem?'

Jonny Searle can be as argumentative as anyone, but this incident was Redgrave's fault. To Redgrave, Searle was Postman Pat: Searle had been given Redgrave's post, therefore it was Searle's job to deliver it, rather than try to fulfil his own Olympic aspirations.

'In Atlanta, I got myself into a right state,' admitted Redgrave. 'I would describe it as "irrational panic". I told myself, "This is terrible. I just can't go out there and race." It always hits me when I'm outside the boat: When I get in it, I'm in my element. I know what I'm doing. I know the score. Deep down, you know that when you're in that Olympic final, rowing side by side with the Australians, there is no way they're going to beat you. That's the frame of mind you've got to get yourself into.'

At Sydney, rowing in the four, he was more 'himself', whoever he was. He and Foster would chat, make 'stupid' observations and swap old unfunny jokes – anything to avoid the real issue of what the hell they were doing there in the first place.

At 28, James Cracknell, youthful in experience if not in years, was an Olympic 'virgin' who had missed Barcelona and Atlanta owing to injury and illness. He coped by blocking out the world with his personal stereo system, lying or sitting stern-faced listening to *Blood, Sugar, Sex, Magik* by the Red Hot Chilli Peppers, his favourite psych-up album, whose aggressive, heavy, funky sound, very strong rhythm and almost-shouted vocals helped induce the mood he wanted.

Foster hid his nerves behind his sunny disposition. 'I get nervous an hour before a race,' he says. 'It is not so much the pain that someone else is going to inflict on you that makes you nervous, as the pain you are about to inflict on yourself. During a race, a devil sits on each shoulder. One whispers, "Why hurt yourself? Why don't you stop? You can stop if you like. Lay down your oar and the pain will go away." The other devil whispers, "Ignore him. You've worked hard to get this far. Push yourself now and you'll have this prize for ever." Hopefully the right devil will win.'

Now, Foster's 'wrong' devil began playing up. *Why do this to yourself? You don't do it for the money. You do it for fun. If for fun, why this agony? That's rowing for you, stress versus boredom. Fool, give it up. Come back and do it tomorrow. Get a life.*

Foster couldn't help visualising the race in flash-forwards. It always seemed agonisingly tough and close, but the outcome was always hazy. He and Cracknell had studied form and pored over every frame of the video footage of the heats and semi-finals. Their main rivals, the Italians and Australians, didn't worry them so much as how much the race would hurt, and how much of an argument those two devils would have before the 'right' devil won.

No contest, thought Foster. He wasn't going to hold back, not even 0.1 per cent. 'I had confidence in my abilities. I was lucky to be in my position. *Okay*, you think, *I don't* want *to be here. But then, were you an ordinary person who'd put himself through what I'd put myself through, you'd be mad not to see it out. And I'd much rather be in the British boat than the Italian or Australian.'*

9.25 a.m.

An Olympic final is not the sort of thing you're late for, so with one hour and five minutes to go before the race, the crew were standing by. They went on a gentle 1.5 kilometre jog to jolt the heart as part of their race-day warm-up. Foster began to run, but stopped after five strides. His knee had gone. He'd almost forgotten about his sore knee. Strange how his catalogue of ailments rose to the big occasion with almost tidal predictability.

'Just walk,' said Redgrave, sensing something amiss with Foster. Among many things left unsaid, Foster's physical frailties were the least mentioned of the lot. Crew protocol meant it was possible to be 'in the same boat' as your crew-mates without letting on about certain personal matters, because each of the crew had his own off-the-record off-the-water challenges, mainly to do with health and nerves, besides the bigger crew challenge of winning. Cracknell's might have been falling ill, as he'd done at Atlanta, or catching a crab (when your oar gets stuck in the water at the point of extraction) fifty metres from the line. Foster's worry was a very immediate physical thing that he'd tried to hide from the crew – except that, of course, no one could have failed to spot the physio's bed hastily throw up in the crew's apartment. And now here was Redgrave surmising Foster's alarm.

After five minutes of walking, the pain in Foster's knee abated. The crew timed their jog to coincide with the final of the coxless pairs, in which Greg Searle and Ed Coode, their training partners and ex-crew-mates, were British medal hopes. Having led for three-quarters of the race, Searle and Coode were overhauled by what seemed a suicidal charge by the French pair of Michel Andrieux and Jean-Christophe Rolland, who took the rate up to 44-plus at an improbable distance from the finishing line. The French scraped home first, followed by Americans Ted Murphy and Sebastian Bea, and then by one-time favourites, the 'oarsome' oarsman James Tomkins and Matthew Long from Australia. Foster's heart sank as he watched the British pair being rowed down inch by inch, but his 'override mechanism' cut in to prevent further distraction.

By the time the four had jogged back to the finishing line, they heard the tannoy blaring out the result.

I'll do the 'feeling sorry for them' bit later, thought Foster. The realisation that the British pair hadn't won a medal at all sharpened Foster's steely sense of determination. *That won't happen to us*, he thought.

9.55 a.m.

Once again, the crew stood by. Redgrave and Foster gave their non-comic joke routine a final run-through. Redgrave would say something; Foster would laugh. Foster would reply; Redgrave would be polite enough to laugh back. Neither of them would make a stand-up comic, but laughter broke the tension.

As oarsmen, however, they were among the greatest in history. Once they were boated and locked into a familiar rhythm and sequence of events, it was almost a relief to be in their element. They paddled off in pairs, first stern pair, then bow pair. It was quiet on the water, except for the rising harangue of their thumping hearts, the sound of the blades chopping into the water and the bubbles whooshing beneath them. Sanctuaried in their routine, the crew paddled up the loop, joined the course, and continued paddling beyond the

Start into a basin, where they practised a couple of bursts. They were aware of other crews warming up, but knew not to be distracted. A couple of shot glances were enough.

All six coxless fours had to be at the Start and ready to race two minutes before the 'off'. With four minutes to go, the British four positioned themselves correctly, with stern in place and bows pointing up the 2000 metre course. There was nothing more to do, except remove T-shirts, which wasted twenty seconds, and wait, in an agony of nerves.

We all start level, thought Foster. *No one has an advantage. We've all done exactly the same training, we're all of roughly the same strength, height, weight and technical ability. It comes down to who wants it more. There will come a point, very soon after the Start, when it will hurt and I'll want to stop. Then I must prove to myself that I really do want Olympic gold and that I'm not just talking myself up by saying so . . .*

'Two minutes!' called the official starter from his tower.

A clog popped out of the water and secured the six bows of the coxless fours, aligning them exactly 2000 metres from the Finish. The crew, especially Redgrave, who steered via strings and pulleys that linked the rudder to one of his feet, had no fears about not starting straight. They checked their gates for the zillionth time. Foster patted Redgrave's foot and Pinsent's back.

'Have a good one.'

There was just the crew and the opposition: twenty-four terrified men pinned in position, awaiting their fate, knowing that the race would not start until the dot of 10.30 a.m. Foster reckoned he could cope with this situation better than most. 'If I'm smiling and they look nervous,' he thought, 'that's an advantage.'

'USA, ready? Slovenia, ready? Great Britain, ready? Australia, ready? . . . Italy, ready? New Zealand, ready? . . . ATTENTION!! . . .'

2

No More 'If Onlys'

How very different the Atlanta coxless four had been. Foster was the only survivor of that excitingly unpredictable boat. His crew-mates had been Rupert Obholzer and the Searle brothers, Greg and Jonny. Obholzer, a driven perfectionist sometimes mistaken for a spluttering volcano, often clashed with Jonny Searle, another perfectionist who was never sure which ideal to strive for, but packed a hell of a temper. Greg Searle, more relaxed and cleaner cut than his dreadlocked brother, inspired respect because he was one of the few oarsmen who could match Matthew Pinsent in the gym and on the ergometer (at which he was the world record holder over 2000 metres), which made him one of the top-rated oarsmen in the world.

The four knew each other perhaps too well. The Searles' gold-medal-winning row in the coxed pairs final at Barcelona had lit up the Olympic regatta: with 10 metres to go, they had inched past the famed Abbagnale brothers. However many times you rewind the video, you still can't believe how they could possibly still win when lying third with 500 metres to go.

The Searles and Obholzer had rowed together at Hampton Grammar School, and had joined Foster as junior internationals in 1987. The Searles knew exactly how to wind each other up, and often did. Jonny Searle was especially volatile. For no obvious reason, he would descend into a catatonic state of pure rage as his blood fizzed and boiled. You could almost see smoke coming off him. On a couple of occasions, in training, he decided that he'd had enough and jumped ship in mid-outing. Curiously, it happened during really good outings. He would begin the outing with something bugging him, like a loose comment that someone had slipped him or a bad day at work (he was a City lawyer). As the outing progressed, he'd get it into his head that the rest of the crew weren't trying hard enough to make it even better, and so he'd get more and more frustrated, until . . . *The world's against me, I'm going to jump out*. He felt a prat long before he lit the water.

When seated next to each other, Jonny Searle and Rupert Obholzer sometimes behaved like inert chemicals that exploded when mixed. Just before the 1994 World Championships, the four had been training on Lake Seminole, a massive crocodile-infested water near Gainsville, in Georgia. One kilometre from shore, the crew were doing some pieces of work. The first two had gone well. For the third, they discussed whether to wind the rate up towards the end. Jonny Searle, on fire to go for it, was outvoted. So they set off, rating 28 strokes a minute. With forty-five seconds to go, Jonny, sitting at three, could contain himself no longer, and tried to take the rate up to 38. Greg Searle, rowing at two, went with him. Obholzer, at stroke, the sternmost seat in the boat whose occupant sets the rate and rhythm, held at 28. The crew fell apart. Chaos ensued. Words flew. Obholzer erupted.

'I'VE TAKEN THIS SHIT FROM YOU SINCE SCHOOL!' Obholzer screamed at Jonny Searle. 'IT'S F***ING RIDICU-

LOUS!' He undid his feet, turned round and leapt on Searle. Meanwhile Greg Searle, pinning back his brother's arm to stop the brawl, merely succeeded in allowing Obholzer a free shot. Steve Gunn, their coach, who taught biology at Hampton Grammar, was following in a launch. Gunn went off too.

'I've never seen anyone so angry,' says Foster. 'Everyone immediately stopped fighting, and skulked back to their seat.' Greg Searle and Foster rowed the boat home. Back on shore, Jonny Searle and Rupert Obholzer strode off towards opposite points of the compass. Ten minutes later they regathered and exchanged apologies.

In 1996 it was Greg Searle's turn to fall out with Obholzer over the non-question of who took the blades from the boathouse to the water's edge. Jonny Searle, watching the fracas, struggled to prevent himself doubling up in hysterics. 'Now I know why, whenever I really get heated up, you lot always laugh at me,' he said. 'I now see that it looks incredibly funny.' Training outings were often so bad-tempered that, before Atlanta, it was decided Foster should row at stroke, steer the boat and give the calls, for the simple reason that no one else could be trusted not to make snide remarks.

The Atlanta four's pre-Games performances at regattas were as volatile as the crew's temperament. Driven on negative energy, they revelled in underdog status, unlike the more confident Sydney four. During a 2000 metre race, any result was possible, from any position, and at any time. In the Olympic year, their early-season form was shocking. At a long-distance time trial in Boston, Lincolnshire, they finished fourth, beaten by two *lightweight* fours and one *coxed* four, an appalling result; but they prided themselves on getting it right on the day, an attitude that crews with poor early-season form often adopt. At one point, it seemed they would be vindicated. At training camp in early July '96, they rowed a 2000 metre piece flat out against the lightweight four and the pair (Pinsent and Redgrave). 'The four had wound us up,' says Foster. 'We overtook them after 300 metres and wiped the floor with them. We finished in under 5 minutes 50 seconds, a very fast time. We'd beaten Matt and Steve on percentages. That was a big moment for us – and them. We'd won by a chunk. They were worried. That was our best row. Grobler put a lot of faith in this piece.'

At Atlanta the coxless four were co-favourites. On the day of the final, Redgrave and Pinsent's pairs race preceded the four's. 'The worst moment was just before we got boated,' says Foster. 'It's hands-on at such-and-such a time, and with five minutes to go you're there and waiting, having left nothing to chance. If an earthquake occurred between your leaving the changing rooms and reaching the boat, you'd still make it. As we waited by the boat, "God Save the Queen" struck up, so we knew Steve and Matthew had won. As we pushed off, they paddled languorously past us with their gold medals. To be fair, they had tried to avoid us. It was the last thing we wanted to see. Not that we wanted them to lose, but in terms of our preparation it conveyed the wrong message psychologically. We needed to feel in some way that we were fighting *against* something.'

The final of the coxless fours ignited the Olympic regatta. After the usual frantic start, the crews settled down more or less level, and held their positions throughout most of the race. At 1500 metres Foster remembers looking across at the field and seeing all the crews still level. All the medals were up for grabs. Between 1250 and 1750 metres gone, Australia put in their 'gold medal 500', took half a length off the field and clung on to it. Australia's 'Oarsome Foursome' won its second successive Olympic gold medal in the coxless fours. In the scramble for minor placings, France managed to squeeze their bows ahead of Great Britain.

When you mount an Olympic medal-winners' rostrum, the

question of the correct etiquette for the facial expression that you wear is not one to which many athletes give much thought. Any superstar who wins gold having expected to do so will be, above all, mightily relieved. A lesser athlete who expects to come nowhere and finds himself thrust on to the podium will be delirious, especially when the drugs tests show negative. If you expected gold but win silver, what face then? A sportingly prolonged rictus, perhaps. What face for bronze? Perhaps a downward tilt of the head, a philosophical drawing back of the sides of the mouth and a resigned 'not-my-day' shrug – accessorised with a pronounced limp.

These thoughts flitted through Foster's mind as he sat slumped in the stroke seat. If one's feelings about any achievement equal Dream plus Hope plus Expectation minus Reality, with a low score indicating joy and a high one indicating sorrow, Foster's was higher than he'd hoped for; but one should be delighted to win any hue of Olympic medal, he concluded, so, grinning, he mounted the rostrum. In unsporting contrast, Obholzer and the Searles glowered thunderously, unable to hide their frustration.

'The other three came across very badly,' says Foster. 'That's not how you should act. Standing on a medal rostrum, you throw on the mask. You are supposed to be celebrating, and acknowledging your supporters. People had come a long way to support us. I felt duty-bound to acknowledge their cheers. I am no stickler for etiquette, except on a medal rostrum. It would wind me up when, in the Sydney four, James and sometimes Matthew didn't remove their glasses on the rostrum, but simply pushed them on top of their heads. Their glasses spent more time on top of their heads than in front of their eyes. A George Michael tribute or a case of sensitive moles?'

Foster admits his Atlanta smile was forced. 'We had failed to rise to the big occasion.' Just 0.91 seconds split gold and bronze medals. There were no recriminations or post-mortems. Rupert Obholzer remembers the last stroke as being 'almost non-existent' ('Just look at the video!'). Far from surging across the line, the boat had drifted, carried by its own momentum. One of the crew, hearing the electronic *blip!* as the Australian bows crossed the line, had stopped pulling, an instinctive reaction when going for gold in a tight race (before praying). This may have accounted for the difference between silver and bronze.

The crew might have done worse, of course. Third, fourth and fifth places were as tightly bunched as first, second and third. Foster has a photograph showing Australia, France, Great Britain, Slovenia, Romania and Italy crossing the line in that order, separated by less than one boat's length. 'We couldn't have expected better,' he says, 'but we had hoped for more.' As 'Advance Australia Fair' grated in his ears, Foster vowed that everything he'd do in the next four years would be aimed at promoting himself a few feet to the right, so that in Sydney, on 23 September 2000, he would stand in the middle of that rostrum. Likewise three Italian, two French, two Slovenian and one Romanian oarsmen from that coxless fours final would go on to contest the Sydney coxless fours.

Ironically, a few minutes before Foster was steeling his resolve, Redgrave had gasped his now immortal line, 'That's it. I've had enough. If anyone sees me go near a boat ever again, they have my permission to shoot me.'

In retrospect, Atlanta wasn't a failure, although it felt like it at the time. The British four were never a certainty for gold. 'Had we raced that race ten times over, we'd have won seven,' says Foster. 'Our row was tactically flawed. We let other crews get ahead and had to work hard in mid-race to claw back. We'd planned a 20 stroke burn with 750 metres to go, but had saved ourselves for it. With 900 metres to go, we were over a length down, and had to raise the rate to 44 to claw back.

There was nothing left in the tank for the last 500 metres. Had we not planned on that 750-metres-to-go burn, maybe we'd have raced harder earlier on.'

The race showed how much easier it is to lose a final than win it. In order to win, so many hundreds of different things have to go right, not just on the day but during the years of training beforehand. Foster admitted to slackness in certain areas. Several 'if onlys' hung in the air. If only he'd trained harder in 1994; if only the crew weren't so inconsistent; if only they hadn't picked Canada for their pre-Games training camp, where the weather had been poor. Shocked by the heat and humidity of Atlanta, the crew struggled during five of their last seven days' preparation.

These and other considerations fuelled Foster's desire. He wanted no more 'if onlys'. He could, and ultimately did, become more professional. If, in the final reckoning, he put himself on the line and did everything in his power, and still won bronze in Sydney, that would be different from the Atlanta bronze. 'But I would far rather swap our most exciting race in Atlanta for the most boring victory in Sydney. The differences between the Atlanta and Sydney fours were not great, perhaps 1 or 2 per cent of the whole picture, but enough to make the difference.'

Given the choice of continuing with the Searles and Obholzer post-Atlanta, Foster probably would have declined. 'Too implosive. The crew would have broken up. Besides, Jonny had a job, and faded away from the top level. Rupert retired to be a doctor. Greg went into the single scull.'

As Foster hit the Olympic Village at Atlanta, and the Redgrave family fled south for a break in Orlando, Steve Redgrave was already plotting a bullet-proof volte-face. The lure of yet more gold, to say nothing of solvency and immortality, was proving irresistible. Atlanta had disappointed Redgrave. 'It wasn't as good as some games I'd been to,' he said, 'and people were saying that Sydney would be the best ever, and the best ever would seem like a good time to end your career. I felt I was just about young enough to go there and win.'

On the flight home, Foster and Redgrave sat next to each other. The body language spoke volumes. Foster's smile said, 'Well done'; Redgrave's shrugs, nods and raised eyebrows said, 'Well done for, er, "winning" bronze, but I know how you feel' (Redgrave had won a bronze in the coxed pair at the Seoul Olympics). Much was left unsaid. The thongs of affection that bound their relationship were hidden within a basic mutual understanding and awareness that excused them from vocal expression.

3

The 'Fab Four'

Being Britain's only gold medallists at Atlanta foisted a degree of public accountability on Redgrave and Pinsent. Only a handful of fans greeted their return, but the celebrity bandwagon revving up around the corner soon hove into sight. For the next four months, Redgrave was peddled hard round the prime-time television studios. Most of it was low-level stuff: judging a washing-up liquid competition with Nanette Newman, winning a special *Gladiators* contest, helping out with the Lottery draw, and being wooed by Shirley Bassey, Bruce Forsyth and Noel Edmonds. He and Pinsent lunched with the Queen and Prince Philip. Redgrave was subjected to *This is Your Life* and upgraded from MBE to CBE in the New Year's honours. He was even named Brain of the Year by the Brains Trust, who unanimously chose him in preference to Bill Gates, Anatoly Karpov (World Chess Champion), Jacques Cousteau (oceanographer) and Professor Deepak Chopra (Director of the Institute for Mind, Body, Medicine and Human Potential) on the grounds that twenty years of continual training was a Herculean triumph of the mind. Qualities attributed to his 'profile of genius' were his outstanding vision, desire, faith, commitment, planning, persistence, and endurance, knowledge of subject, imagination, positive attitude, tactical thinking, strategic thinking, creativity and flexibility and energy. Only eight days of his four-month break were *not* spent doing promotional work of one sort or another.

Pinsent had his moments too. A man recognised him shopping in Henley, and stared, open-mouthed. 'How's your gold medal?' he blurted out.

'It's doing very well, thank you,' replied Pinsent. 'Pretty much like any other gold medal, really.'

Pinsent had no inkling of Redgrave's plans. They had parted with a firm handshake and a look in the eye. He had assumed Redgrave had retired. One day in September, Pinsent turned up at the Leander Club to meet Grobler. 'I hadn't spoken to anybody since Atlanta,' recalled Pinsent. 'I didn't even know Jürgen's plans, whether he even wanted to continue to coach; but whatever happened, it was going to be without Steve. The first thing he tells me is Steve's thinking of carrying on.' It would take more than a feather to knock down 6 feet 5 inches Pinsent, but this came as a seismic shock. 'I remember telling him he was wrong, but I went straight to the phone to call Steve and he told me he was thinking about it.'

Although Redgrave returned to the fray in December 1996 in 'terrible shape', he felt the time off had refreshed him. A hunger of the soul had returned. Beckoning him on was a hand grasping the Olympic torch. Only when halfway through his first endurance circuit and finding the going tough did he wonder, 'What the hell am I doing here?'

Pinsent was adamant he didn't want to continue in a pair. Rowing in a pair is inherently stressful. There is no one to share the tension with except your partner. The single scull is even worse. Marnie McBean, a Canadian oarswoman who won two gold medals at Barcelona – in an eight and a pair – later took up single sculling. She described it as the loneliest boat in the sport. Many oarsmen, Redgrave among them, aspired to win gold in the single scull. She achieved this, but said afterwards that it was like going to see a really good film on your own. You had no one to share it with. That's what rowing in small boats is like. It's going to the cinema on your own.

So a coxless four was mooted as the British flagship. This seemed an excellent idea, and a heroically sporting one too. The Australians, the 'Oarsome Foursome', had won the coxless fours at both the Barcelona and Atlanta Games. They would no doubt want to defend their title before their home crowd at Sydney. The Oarsome Foursome vs Redgrave & Co. would top the bill at the Olympic regatta as a titanic head-to-head. Besides, as Pinsent once said, if winning was easy, it would be no fun.

The four would contain the strongest, fittest and most technically gifted oarsmen, two apiece from bow side and stroke side (oarsmen tend to row on one side of the boat or the other, and rarely switch over): same high goal, just a different route to the top, and not an easier one, albeit a few seconds quicker in the final reckoning.

While each seat would be properly trialled for, it was obvious that two of them would be amply filled by Pinsent and Redgrave. Grobler had minimum physical requirements in strength, height, weight and reach that he demanded of aspiring international oarsmen. Redgrave, grazed-knuckled and with a 6 feet 4 inch, 105 kilogram frame (that's without his four gold and one bronze Olympic medals), was the very pattern of a likely rowing superstar. Strong but not strongest, fit but not fittest, technically good but no maestro, he scored in the mental department. He had succeeded thanks to a combination of hard work, professionalism, single-mindedness, stubbornness and a remarkable ability to flout health scares, accidents and medical adversity in general, rather than by natural talent. Single-mindedness is a great rarity among human beings, but Redgrave combined it with a self-confidence, a sense of mission, even of destiny, shored up by a compelling faith, and – most of all – the will and stamina that sifts the great from the gifted. 'Redgrave crews are not always a pretty sight,' wrote Chris Dodd, then the *Guardian*'s rowing correspondent, 'but when it comes to moving boats, he is a prime mover, at one time *the* prime mover.' His 'characteristic slouch powering a boat through the water' had dominated international regattas for almost twenty years.

Besides his harvest of four Olympic gold and one Olympic bronze medals, he had six World Championship titles, three Commonwealth titles and seventeen medals won at Henley Royal Regatta. A sharp-witted philosophical soul when relaxed, he transformed, Hyde-like, into a brooding hulk of Heathcliffian intensity when immersed in his sport. He had subjected his body to intense exertion and exhaustion, stretching his own gifts of heroic aspiration to breaking point, with all the risks entailed. His medical record was rich in pathological instances, and could merit its own supplement in the *Lancet*. He was the most determined, most respected, most impressive and potentially most arthritic man in sport.

'Steve is as good as he is because he has worked at it,' says Foster. 'He is physically very impressive, but not naturally a five-times Olympic gold-medallist. He is a four-times Olympic gold-medallist who has worked very hard, and is very professional. He isn't superhuman. He suffers like the rest of us. If it's a tough day, he struggles, which makes him more exceptional or more worthy of respect.'

Redgrave was also a household name in Great Britain for having somehow eluded the BBC Sports Personality of the Year, an annual gong voted for by television viewers on which sports personality they'd admired the most. Measurable achievement and sheer talent hardly counted. The award was inherently skewed towards populist sports – football, rugby, motor sport and cricket – but nonetheless carried prestige for its longevity. All Redgrave had to show for being arguably Britain's most achieving athlete was a huge mortgage and a numismatic paperweight museum. As a nation, Britain prefers to look down on people, even its own citizens. It warms to brilliant failures, not outstanding successes. Redgrave's flaw was, in a sense, not having one, or not one that people could relate to. He had no show-stopping dysfunctionality or redeeming vice such as made the likes of George Best, John McEnroe and Mike Tyson such compelling figures.

He had taken up rowing at 14 after Francis Smith, his English teacher at Marlow High School, had spotted his large hands and feet. 'He figured that if you had those at 14, you'd grow up to be a big, powerful person. I was one of those people at the time, and at the time there couldn't have been many better things than going out on the river during school time. During our first season we won all seven of the events we entered and thought we were God's gift to rowing.'

When international coaches asked him to break up his school's four to row in a junior international eight, he refused. Those coaches exacted bitter-sweet revenge by ignoring him at the 1979 World Junior Championships in Moscow, where Redgrave entered in the single scull.

'Nobody would talk to me in Moscow,' he said. 'The athletes were OK, but the coaches, the people in the system, wouldn't. The national coach of the juniors never spoke to me once while I was out there. The guy that drove the trailer felt sorry for me and looked after me instead.'

Elimination from the single scull in those World Junior Championships left an indelible weal on his psyche. Having no French, the then lingua franca of international rowing, Redgrave was so scared of missing his heat, that, instead of warming up, he sat on the Start and waited for other scullers whom he recognised to arrive. He started the race cold. He could never forget the West German sculler who beat him –

by what distance and in what time – and the Czech sculler who matched him stroke-for-stroke and inched him into third place and failure. 'You need to know how easy it is *not* to be best, to be best,' he said.

Mike Spracklen, an early mentor, spotted Redgrave and entertained hopes of his becoming a great single sculler. 'Steve knew exactly what he wanted,' Spracklen once said, 'and how he was going to do it . . . No one could pull the wool over his eyes, no one.' The single scull, an inherently solitary discipline, suited his temperament: 'Steve's ideal life would be never to go out,' Ann Redgrave once told *Hello!* 'He would love to live in the middle of nowhere, with no contact whatsoever with human beings.'

His first real success, however, came in the coxed four that he stroked to gold at the Los Angeles Olympics in 1984. 'It was kind of awe-inspiring for me to sit in the bow seat and try to keep up with this power which I hadn't felt in a boat before,' said Martin Cross, Redgrave's crew-mate. 'There was a kind of brutality about it. Steve is prepared to row with people and be a team member, and that's a very endearing side to his character, though it's not always evident, because he's so single-minded in his attitude to rowing.' Dr Richard Budgett, another crew-mate from that Los Angeles coxed four, hailed Redgrave as 'an astonishing competitor. Other people have good or bad days, but Steve wins every time. He is not arrogant; he is absolutely, if quietly, sure that he is the best.'

Pinsent exceeded Grobler's physical template by a mile, but was a very different animal. Whereas Redgrave, the dyslexic builder's son with one O level in Woodwork, had had to choose between rowing and obscurity, Pinsent, the vicar's son, had had to decide between rowing and cricket. With his born-to-rule Eton-and-Oxford education, easy manner, air of effortless superiority and imposing bearing, he made a splendid ambassador for the British Establishment and melted into the background whenever Redgrave was grilled about rowing being an elitist sport. At Oxford he read Geography and the *Daily Telegraph*, and rowed in three Boat Races, twice a winner. There was talk he might one day enter politics.

He lived alone in Henley and rarely visited London. His chief interests seemed to be sleeping, the cinema and golf. He was mildly annoyed when the local golf club, having made Redgrave a life member, merely placed him at the head of the queue of would-be paying members. He once tried to take Redgrave up in his helicopter, but found they exceeded the maximum permissible payload.

'I wasn't particularly good at sport until I was 17,' he said. 'I wasn't really big for my age until I was 16. Then it took me another year to get used to the technique; but once I'd got that I became much more competitive.'

In 1990, when Redgrave was interviewing prospective pairs partners for the Barcelona Olympics, Pinsent wasn't the obvious candidate in terms of strength and experience. At 19, he was a first-year undergraduate at Oxford. Had he seat-raced for the right to row with Redgrave, eight and a half years his senior, he might not have emerged as favourite. Redgrave, however, with his knack of spotting potential winners, sensed something about Pinsent, while Matthew's strength and freakish ability to work aerobically was already being cooed about among the old heavies in the Floating Stand at Henley Royal Regatta.

'I was obviously pretty nervous,' he said of teaming up with Redgrave. 'But I was also aware that I wanted to make it an equal partnership and that it was never going to work if it wasn't. But it was apparent within the first couple of weeks of being together that it was going to go well, and it wasn't a problem mentally.'

A little over a year later, Redgrave and Pinsent were World Champions. Since then, Pinsent had gone on to win two Olympic gold medals with Redgrave at Barcelona and Atlanta.

Now, just shy of his thirtieth birthday, he had overtaken Redgrave in the gym and was leaving him behind. He carried the flame as the top-rated oarsman in Britain and arguably the world. At 108 kilograms and 6 feet 5 inches tall, he was certainly one of the heaviest and tallest. However, there was always a feeling within the squad that his limits had never been fully probed and that, being so naturally gifted, he didn't have to try as hard as the others.

The two other seats in the coxless four were some of the most prized pieces of furniture in the sport. Besides Pinsent, Martin Cross and Dr Richard Budgett, the only other oarsman to have rowed with Redgrave at the Olympics was Andy Holmes in the coxed four at Los Angeles, and the coxed and coxless pairs at Seoul.

Grobler combed the list of candidates. He was looking for a certain type of giant that would hit his physiological jackpot. Rowing is rated among the most testing sports, both aerobically and anaerobically. Sports-medicine doctors classify it alongside water polo, boxing, skiing and ice hockey as 'high intensity', with 'high dynamic and static demands' requiring, some say, the heart and lungs of a marathon runner and the strength of a rugby forward. The resting pulse of an elite oarsman is about 38 (the average for adult human beings is 70). Foster's was 34. Within twenty seconds of the start of a race it would shoot up to 190. Grobler soon identified a shortlist of Greg Searle, Tim Foster, Rupert Obholzer, Richard Hamilton, Ben Hunt-Davis, Bobby Thatcher and James Cracknell.

In late 1996 Foster had put Sydney temporarily out of his mind, dropped out of the squad and gone up to Oxford University briefly to read Social Sciences. Academic studies never wasted much of his time, his sole aim being the Boat Race – he even lived in the rat-infested University boat house – and he was the star turn of the Oxford University rowing squad that year. One autumn day, Grobler dropped by, ostensibly to watch Oxford train but actually to sound Foster out about rowing in a coxless four with Redgrave, Pinsent and Greg Searle, rather like a latter-day Smiley sizing up potential spooks.

Foster doubted that this ad hoc coalition of super-athletes would ever make it down the slipway. Pinsent and Searle were like kryptonite to each other. They could hardly bear to be in the same room, never mind the same crew. Pinsent vs Searle ran deeper than merely Golden Boy 1 vs Golden Boy 2. It evoked the *hiss! spit!* rivalries of Eton College vs Hampton Grammar, and Leander Club vs Molesey Boat Club. In 1992 Molesey-based Greg Searle and his brother Jonny beat Pinsent and Redgrave in the main Amateur (ahem!) Rowing Association (ARA) pairs trial, and vied with them throughout that pre-Barcelona Olympic season. It later emerged that Redgrave was suffering from colitis, but there was always a sense of an unresolved rivalry hanging about the squad as to which of the two stroke-side oarsmen – Pinsent or Greg Searle – was the greater. Searle diplomatically quashed any idea of trialling for the four, claiming it was too risky. He fancied his chances in the single scull.

As for Foster, uppermost in Grobler's mind was an ergometer test Foster had done earlier that year while training for Atlanta (Grobler tended to think of people in terms of ergometer scores). Foster had clocked 5 minutes 52 seconds over 2000 metres, ranking him fourth in the squad in a faster time than his coaches had expected. Grobler never witnessed the test, but later, when told, said, 'Wow!', slapped Foster on the back and shook his hand. That was a key moment. 'Jürgen ranks physicality very highly,' says Foster. 'Until then, he knew I had boat-moving skills, but thought I couldn't pull the skin off rice pudding.'

That autumn day, Grobler never did stay to watch Oxford train.

Foster wasn't so sure about joining Redgrave and Pinsent.

Before Atlanta he'd watched them and been appalled by their grimly serious public personas. Their assumed air of dour professionalism counted against them. At press conferences they'd been portrayed as not enjoying their rowing and regarding it purely as a job in which training was a necessary chore. People found them morose. It was as if Redgrave were presenting a ransom demand: hand over more cash or I destroy my chance of a medal.

To Foster rowing was more than a job. Playing about on the river, being within a group, going to the gym and chatting with mates were things he loved. 'I could imagine getting an office job and not getting any reward other than money,' he said. 'As an oarsman, the money was shocking; but the rewards were far greater than anything money could buy.'

Appearances deceived in Foster. Laid-back, earringed and with a penchant for flowing Kurt Cobain hair-dos (a handy sail in tailwinds), Spandau Ballet, Tottenham Hotspur and tartan trousers, he looked more like the 'occasional rock musician' that graced his CV than an Olympic athlete. A much-decorated junior oarsman, he was considered one of the sport's finest technicians and was the first British oarsman to win two Junior World Championship gold medals (1987, 1988). Somehow, thanks to a combination of accident, ill luck and injury, he'd missed out on striking gold as a senior. Four bronzes and a silver at Olympic and Senior World Championship level were no compensation.

He took up rowing on the Great Ouse at Bedford Modern School aged 14, in January 1984. 'The school didn't play football,' he says, 'and rugby was too regimented. My elder brother had rowed and hated it. I didn't immediately take to it. It was an escape. You could hide behind the island.' That summer he intended to play cricket, but was surprised and encouraged to be picked to row in an eight for the regatta season.

Competing at the national rowing championships in his

debut summer, he finished last in a Junior Under-14 quadruple scull. After playing rugby for one term, he resumed the oar and won his first open event: Junior Under-15 coxed fours at Cambridge Sprint Regatta in '85. 'Mum and Dad cheered from the bank,' he says. 'The race lasted two minutes. It took me two hours to explain it to them. I've still got the tankard.' Foster was plucked to row in Bedford Modern's top eight, alongside 18-year-olds.

In 1987 he trialled for the junior international squad, cutting a dash in his rugby shorts. His training had consisted of paddling the 1800 metres as far as the next lock, and racing back, five times a week. As training programmes went, it was good ol' tried-and-tested muddling through at its finest. Foster kept quiet when his co-trialists from Hampton Grammar School, a crèche of junior international oarsmen and rowing blues, bragged about twelve training sessions each week – twice a day during the week and once a day at weekends.

Foster swept the board. He won every race. Still in rugby shorts, he was tossed among the cream of junior oarsmen. In the final race to select the British junior coxless four, the top-rated four of boys from Marlow High School and Hampton Grammar raced against a four containing Foster, Toby Hessian, Charlie Holmes and Paul Dilkes. 'We won,' says Foster. 'Myself, Jonny Searle, Toby Hessian and Rupert Obholzer were eventually selected and put in a four. Later that year, we won a gold medal at the World Junior Championships.' Foster won a second junior gold medal the following year pairing with Pinsent.

Foster was the odd man out of the squad. At 6 feet 3 inches, he was tall enough but, weighing 'only' 86 kilograms, was too light (Grobler demanded 91 kilograms). His long limbs but small frame earned him the nickname 'No Body'. When Grobler arrived in Britain, Foster was training with a refusenik element within the national squad that was based at the

University of London boathouse in Chiswick and at Molesey Boat Club in Surrey. Grobler worked with the remainder of the squad at the Leander Club, having been assured he had the best men. At training camp in 1991, Foster and his colleagues set out to destroy this notion. In an illustration of Newton's laws of equal and opposite forces, they did the opposite to what Grobler did, and Grobler did the opposite to what they did.

Grobler looked Foster up and down as if he were making a suit for him, and shook his head. He didn't rate Foster and said – behind his back – that he wasn't strong enough. There was a bleak impasse. 'I remember sitting in an aeroplane wedged between Jürgen and Martin Cross, my partner in a pair, all three of us in a line,' says Foster. 'When Jürgen wanted to know how the pair was going, he leant forward to ask Martin, cutting me out of the conversation. Very strange.' When Foster stroked the eight to a bronze medal in the 1991 World Championships, Grobler finally congratulated him.

At one training camp in Banyoles, site of the 1992 Olympic regatta, there was a strong 'them and us' tension within the squad. The Leander element would get up early and row 20 kilometres, while the London element would lie in and do sprints. Leander felt they had to be seen to be acting 'professionally', whereas the London faction made a point of appearing to be anything but. Foster and his crew deliberately rowed past the boathouse naked, just to show that they were having more fun than the Leander boys were. When one of the Leander boys let slip about Foster being unprofessional, Martin Cross leapt to defend his honour. Greg and Jonny Searle, Molesey stalwarts, were openly subversive, while Cross would refuse to do anything that conformed with anyone's idea of correct procedure. At one squad camp in Nottingham, Foster and Cross were due to go out in a pair early one morning but failed to turn up at the boathouse.

Brian Armstrong, then team manager, stormed into their room to rage at them, to be confronted by Cross, naked, reading a newspaper, and Foster fast asleep.

'I'm reading the paper and Tim's still asleep,' said Cross calmly.

'But everyone else is out on the water training,' spluttered Armstrong.

'Good for them. We'll go out before lunch.'

In 1992 Cross and Foster turned up to the Amateur Rowing Association pairs trial, to have Grobler seed them eighteenth out of eighteen pairs. Cross and Foster delighted in thrashing all comers and only lost out to Redgrave and Pinsent by 0.05 seconds, having just failed to row them down. They finished the trial as the third-ranked pair in the country. At the Barcelona Olympics later that year, Grobler exacted revenge by putting Cross and Foster in the bows of a weak eight. That rankled.

'That was politics,' says Foster. 'The eight was a shambles, only put together six weeks before the Games. We had so many illnesses and injuries that at one point Derek Drinkwater, the ARA boatman and an occasional club rower, had to substitute.'

The upshot of these episodes was that Foster was branded a talented maverick, a reputation which he did nothing to dispel – indeed sought to enhance and polish up whenever possible.

During the 1991 campaign, Foster's eight was briefly graced by a young, keen oarsman who was 'a bit rough around the edges' and had 'very silly hair, virtually shaved off except for a Jonah-Lomu-style frontal crest, but worse'. His name was James Cracknell.

Cracknell's daring coiffures, tattoos and insouciant manner were misleading too. Like Pinsent and Foster, he had tasted Junior World Championship glory by winning gold in the coxless four in 1990. Like Pinsent, he was strong but technically rough. Unlike Pinsent, who got the break of a lifetime by being plucked to pair with Redgrave, Cracknell got the opposite end of the stick and was shoved into the lower echelons of the squad, where he was considered immensely strong but no boat-mover. As Rachel Quarrell, rowing correspondent of the *Daily Telegraph*, put it, 'He could pull an ergometer machine to bits, but the problem for James was that ergos don't float.'

Grobler, seeing in Cracknell shades of the East German hulks he'd once coached, marked him down as a potential stroke of the eight (East German coaches tended to put their strongest man at stroke; English coaches tended to put their most *skilful* man at stroke). Then Cracknell's star began to wane. He failed to be selected for Barcelona owing to a shoulder injury playing rugby. He turned down the role of 'spare man', thinking he'd been unfairly treated, only to be told he'd never row for Britain again. Nothing would spur Cracknell more than a spiteful blazer telling him he'd never row for his country again. He stormed back into the gym, banged weights around and tore at the ergometer machines. Between the Barcelona and Atlanta Olympics, he could just about bear seeing Pinsent and Redgrave being treated with kid gloves and cotton wool, but he raged at what he saw as the closed shop of the Atlanta coxless four. 'I was beating that crew on the rowing machine, in the single scull and in a pair,' he says. 'That was harsh. They were a very inconsistent crew.'

Atlanta was his sorriest sporting moment. Tonsillitis ambushed him on the day of the opening ceremony, ironically making him the biggest threat to Redgrave's gold medal hopes in the pair. Walking to lunch one day, his pulse shot to over 120. 'By the time I got back, all the other guys in the apartment had gone,' he said. 'It was like the *Marie Celeste*.' He thought about giving up rowing altogether, then decided to have a last shot at the four. He would take nothing for granted. Every inch of the journey to Sydney would have to be fought for.

Cracknell had previously met Redgrave on a couple of occasions, but under very different circumstances. As an 11-year-old, he had asked Redgrave for his autograph at the World Championships at Nottingham in 1986. Redgrave had refused. Touchingly, he paid Redgrave the compliment of naming one of his goldfish Steve after Redgrave's triumph at Seoul. Cracknell was even coached by Redgrave in a junior pair. Having got boated and pushed off, Cracknell capsized before Redgrave's disbelieving eyes, having forgotten to tighten the gate of his rigger that fastened his oar.

After exhaustive trials conducted over six months in Britain and abroad, three contenders emerged to partner Pinsent and Redgrave: Foster, Cracknell and Bobby Thatcher. Thatcher was dropped at a trial at Hazewinkel in Belgium, leaving just Foster and Cracknell.

'Congratulations,' said Grobler to Cracknell. 'You are in – for now.'

Cracknell might have imagined that Redgrave would outlive Steve the goldfish, but never in his wildest fantasies that his hero would be around long enough for them to row together in a flagship boat bound for the Olympics. It was tempting to assume that it was all a dream and that he'd wake up at any moment.

Rowing is fundamentally a team sport, and this particular team was a motley one: Foster the renegade 1960s-style hippy; Cracknell the earnest, driven perfectionist, who put his life on the line every time he stepped into a boat; Pinsent the sanguine monster, and Redgrave the brooding, phenomenal competitor. But they got along famously. Psychologically and in terms of their abilities, they were well balanced. Foster introduced a scrupulous technical perfectionism, quality control, an indestructible cheeriness and a refusal to make things harder than they were; Cracknell the motivator stood as a rebuke and a reminder of what real desire, enthusiasm and commitment were all about; Redgrave added determination and hard-edged professionalism; while Pinsent put up numbers in the gym that were beyond what anyone else was capable of, yet leaving a suspicion that there was more to come.

'With four Steves in the boat, the crew would tear itself apart,' said Foster. 'Equally, if there were four men like me, we'd probably never get up in the morning. There were never any arguments. I played the role of mediator and pacifier, jumping in and making fun of myself, if there was a heated moment, to defuse "situations".'

'No one has an ego problem,' said Cracknell. 'We all have got faith that the four of us are the best people. That throws confrontation out of the window. The total professionalism of Jürgen also helps.'

The crew was due to be launched before the media in early April 1997. Redgrave's body immediately registered its own protest just as he and his family prepared to depart for a pre-launch break to Spain.

'I'm in agony,' he told his wife one night. As a GP, Ann Redgrave was well placed to make the diagnosis. Her first thought was, 'He's got appendicitis.' Her second thought was, 'This is going to ruin the holiday.'

'You'll be all right,' she said, sending him to bed. She was right on both counts. It was appendicitis. It did ruin the holiday. There followed, in swift succession, ambulance, hospital, operation, fight-back.

Tuesday, 22 April 1997

Ten days after Redgrave's appendectomy, the coxless four was launched with a press conference and photo-opportunity paddle at the Leander Club in Henley-on-Thames, where Redgrave and Pinsent had been based as a pair. Redgrave heeded his consultant's advice not to exercise for three weeks – that's if you turn a blind eye to the cycling, weights sessions, outing and round of golf he'd had with Pinsent in the days just before the launch. It was a wonder he hadn't performed the surgery himself, using a mirror, blunt surgical instrument and medical textbook.

The Leander Club, located just downstream of Henley Bridge, is the sort of club Groucho Marx had in mind when he made his famous quote. Bearing the name of the unfortunate youth who drowned in the Hellespont en route to a tryst with Hero, priestess of Aphrodite, Leander is one of the oldest, most venerated rowing clubs in the world. It was instrumental in developing the sport of rowing in the early nineteenth century, and has maintained its pre-eminence as a centre of excellence in men's heavyweight and, lately, women's rowing.

It runs its own star-spangled squad of elite oarsmen creamed from the top schools, universities and clubs. If the whipped cream of the Leander squad go on to grace the national squad, Redgrave and Pinsent were pure full-fat Chantilly. If a smart boat club can be defined as any structure that doesn't float off with a high tide, Leander is the dog's bollocks. It even has heated boat bays to dry the 'shells' (rowing-speak for sleek racing boats). In some respects, Leander is socially elitist too. The membership – identifiable at regattas by cerise ties and socks – revolves around a public-school–Oxbridge axis. Long-haired Foster and earringed Cracknell were the last people you'd expect to find pulling on the full pinko regalia, which was tantamount to social self-flagellation, although Foster secretly thrilled at the clash of his cerise Leander accessories and his purple University of London blazer. Pinsent was another matter.

At the press conference all eyes locked on to Redgrave and Pinsent. When one journalist asked, 'Wouldn't it have been better to quit now at the top?', Redrave, all steel and ice, replied, 'I am going on to Sydney, and I still expect to go out at the top.' 'But,' persisted the press, 'by the time of the Olympics you'll be 38 and fast approaching relict status.' Redgrave countered by pointing out that the oldest rowing gold medallist was 42 – 'So age isn't a barrier.'

Andy Ripley, the former England rugby international and all-round sportsman who at 50 rowed in the Cambridge University squad in 1997, seemed to confirm this when he reported, 'The exertion is enormous, but it is cumulative rather than explosive . . . In rowing, age isn't such a problem because, like swimming or cycling, you are not supporting your own weight, so there is less strain on your joints.'

Foster and Cracknell, 'the other two', were flipped a couple of sympathy questions about expectations for Sydney. *Eh?* thought Cracknell, whose focus was on the Munich international regatta in three weeks' time, not Sydney in three and a half years'. Ever since 1991 Redgrave and Pinsent had travelled to regattas expecting to win, and had swaggered home laden with gold. The closest Cracknell had ever got to winning senior gold was sixth in the eight in 1993. Here he was, hauled up before the media, under the spotlight, being asked to share his views on winning gold at Sydney. He suddenly realised that international regatta wins and World Championship titles, which to him were elusive prizes winking in the far distance, were to Redgrave and Pinsent merely transitory gongs to be gathered in and cast aside en route to the Big One in Sydney. The implications of rowing with Redgrave and Pinsent sank in immediately. For Cracknell, the honeymoon would be a brief one. The thrill of landing such a high-profile rowing seat was immediately overshadowed by the challenge of hanging on to it.

After the press conference, the four embarked on their debut outing, trailed by the media in a launch and followed by crowds on the bank. Pinsent rowed at stroke, Foster at 3,

Cracknell at 2 and Redgrave at bow. Towpath tourists wondered what all the fuss was about and stopped baby-minders with strollers to ask. The Olympics were still thirty-nine months away, yet here were the world's media lining the river bank like expectant ducks, and hanging off Henley Bridge like gargoyles. This was proof that Redgrave had saved rowing from its amateur ghetto and brought it to the masses, unlike Jack Kelly, six times Diamond Sculls winner at Henley, who had always been more famous for being Princess Grace's father, and unlike Boris Rankov, the most successful rowing blue and winner of six Boat Races, often confused with Boris 'Frankenstein's Monster' Karlov.

Foster and Cracknell were not unaware of their lowly profiles. Neither of them enjoyed lucrative Lombard sponsorship, an MBE or newspapers asking them how they'd vote at the General Election on 1 May. After the outing, Cracknell slipped off to 'sign on'. For Foster, it was bizarre to step into the four. A month earlier he had been a humble student and ex-stroke of a losing Oxford Boat Race crew. Now he was thrust into the public eye for simply turning up to a press conference. He and Cracknell had to smile their way through a barrage of sneering asides. 'I see you've got some big friends now' was a common refrain. There were dark mutterings about them having 'joined the elite', implying that Pinsent and Redgrave were carrying them. The question Cracknell was most often asked was: 'What is it like to race with Steve and Matthew?' The consensus was that Cracknell and Foster were in an invidious position – ignored if they won, blamed if they lost.

Foster also had a sense of déjà vu. He'd been here before, cast as one of the 'other two' in the previous Olympic coxless four when he and Rupert Obholzer had been eclipsed by the Searle Brothers! Now he was billed as one of the 'other two' hod-carriers to Redgrave and Pinsent's monument.

Henley is a picturesque malting town and former port that

straddles the Thames about 35 miles from London. Here, the looming form of Steve Redgrave was as much part of the riverside furniture as the 1786 town bridge and the Angel pub. The modern sport of rowing was born on the mile-and-a-half straight of Henley Reach when the first Oxford vs Cambridge Boat Race took place in 1829, which then begot Henley Regatta in 1839, which became Henley *Royal* Regatta after His Royal Highness Prince Albert (later HRH the Prince Consort) patronised it in 1851.

Depending on the season, the Thames flows between (for the most part) wild and unwalled riverbanks hurriedly and muddily, or peacefully and translucently. On certain days its waters resemble a fine mass of shimmering, metallic, luminous blue. On some evenings it looks like a mirror reflecting the sky from which it seems to issue. In fields and meadows where the grass really is greener, livestock grazes in the shade of mighty trees. One or two properties have boathouses, where an elegant launch or simple punt might be moored. Crowning the reach is James Wyatt's wedding-cake folly (1771) on Temple Island, down by the start of the regatta course. Moving back upstream towards Henley, the famous regatta landmarks – the Barrier (little more than a gate on the towpath), Remenham Farm, Fawley Court, the Remenham Club – ring in the ears of oarsmen worldwide like a drum roll urging them to action.

The river, its idyllic setting and drop-dead views remain essentially unchanged in nearly 200 years. This was the crew's office. They measured the seasons in freezing salmon-pink winter dawns, denuded trees, ice on the loom, then flaming summer days, mists of spiralling gnats, the honk-honk of gin palaces and the annual painstaking construction of the Henley Royal Regatta course, whose booms and piles are erected and dismantled before and after each Royal Regatta in early July.

The only eyesore in this seductively picturesque backdrop

was the Leander Club itself, Pink Sock Central. A clumsy, rambling structure guilty of the worst pebble-dash and mock Tudor solecisms of the Thames Valley subtopia, its bulk was appropriate for a shrine to rowing, but it lacked the grace and elegance of its finest practitioners. Inside, it was a piece of Henley that will be forever Ikea, with awkwardly shaped low-ceilinged rooms. The Leander gym was even worse. With its flocculent dust, peeling paint, exposed polystyrene insulation, sheets of plastic, a torn mottled 'carpet', weights resting on old sofa cushions and ceilings impregnated with the sour smell of stale sweat, all lit by strip lighting that hung by a thread, it would have raised eyebrows at the RSPCA. This cell purged the oarsmen of whatever fripperies of fame came their way, and placed those podium moments in perspective. No one submitting an application for Lottery funds to help redevelop the gym would ever have dared describe it as as rat-gnawed and mouldering as it actually was.

Between late 1997 and early 1999 the Leander Club was redeveloped with help from a Lottery grant. While the work took place, the crew changed in a Portakabin and converted one of the boat bays into a makeshift gym. If you placed a bar weight on the floor, it would roll downhill. In early 1999, a gleaming new gym was unveiled. It made training pure pleasure, until they discovered that some bright spark had forgotten to fit a ventilation system. Training on the ergometer machines, the crew suffered oxygen deprivation. To help stir up the air, Foster brought in a stand-alone fan.

'Oh Tim,' chuckled Grobler, 'you like to row with a tailwind, I think.' It reduced Foster's heart rate by 20 beats a minute.

The crew trained at Leander under the hawk eye of the watch-tapping Grobler. Ever since 1972 Grobler had groomed medal-winning crews at every World Championships and Olympic Games, except Los Angeles in 1984, which the Soviet bloc boycotted. Although he claimed he rowed at the East

German University Championships and could plausibly carry off a tracksuit during training, the closest any member of the squad had got to witnessing his prowess with an oar was in 1994 when Redgrave and Pinsent were invited to compete in the indoor world rowing championships in Boston, USA. Grobler wanted to join them. The only way he could get his travel expenses paid for was if he went as a 'competitor'. His scores never troubled the leader board.

Grobler declared that, in order to win, the crew must up the intensity of their training by 10 per cent compared to the previous Olympiad. Treading water wouldn't do. At every four-year turn of the Olympic wheel, the bar was set higher. Redgrave's winning time in the coxed four in 1984 wouldn't have qualified him for the final of the coxed fours in Seoul in 1988; his gold-medal-winning time in Seoul in the coxless pair wouldn't even have won him a medal in Barcelona 1992. You had to find more every time.

Beginning at 8 a.m., the crew rowed 20 kilometres, equivalent to going from the Leander Club two and a half miles downstream to Hambleden Lock and back two and a half times. At weekends, and during the summer, Henley Reach took on the allure of the Grand Canal in Venice, so to avoid traffic and catch the flat water, the majority of training was done early in the morning.

The next stop would be the Leander gym. Cracknell had his corner, Redgrave and Pinsent had theirs. Redgrave was the cock of the roost. Other squad members stepped aside on the weights and ergometers, having nicely warmed them up for him. There was no formal or official delineation of rank. It was just understood that HRH Redgrave had precedence and took it. Another example of the minute squad pecking order at work was whereabouts you sat in the Leander breakfast room: the closer to the television, the better the oarsman (and the worse the eyesight, in Foster's case); the further away from the television, the more likely you were to be in receipt of a dreaded 'pink postcard' informing you that your services would no longer be required.

Each day, the squad would do four circuits of seventeen different exercises. The exercises were:

Bench pulls, 55 kilograms, 50 repetitions to take no more than 2 minutes
Sit-ups on incline, 10 kilograms, 20 repetitions
Press-ups, 20 repetitions
Knives (throwing feet and arms upwards), 20 repetitions
Rowing on a box, 10 kilograms each hand, 30 repetitions
Dorsal rises, 15 kilograms, 15 repetitions
Bench pulls, 45 kilograms, 30 repetitions, to take no more than one minute
Angels (lie face down, lift arm and leg), 5 kilograms, 20 repetitions
Squat jumps, 30 repetitions
Lateral pulls, 50 kilograms, 20 repetitions
Leg curls, 30 kilograms, 20 repetitions
Side bends, 45 kilograms, 20 repetitions
Step-ups, 50 kilograms, 20 repetitions (10 each leg)
(Chest) Expander, 30 quick strokes.

The 'expander' was a converted chest expander. One end was attached to a wall of the gym, a rowing handle was attached to the other. The action – drawing the handle towards the body – was supposed to represent the finish of the rowing stroke. Anyone who saw Pinsent at the expander would assume he was having some kind of fit. His action was all arms, back and head, but involved minimal movement of the handle, besides the spring bouncing up and down. The squad thought the exercise was laughable. When the expander was accidentally left behind at a rowing training camp, the squad joked that maybe other nations would discover their secret weapon. Grobler was not amused.

The crew would do this fifteen-minute circuit four times, the silence broken only by staccato grunts and the clunk of heavy metal. To the uninitiated, it looked at very best like a fast track to repetitive strain injury.

After the weights, the squad rowed 16 or 20 kilometres on ergometer machines or another 16 kilometres on the water. The day's training was designed to get you to a point of extreme tiredness and keep you there for as long as possible. With a break for breakfast, the day's training could take six hours. It was time on the treadmill: seven days a week, forty-nine weeks of each year. That was all there was to it. The scenic backdrop might change – the crew was forever going off on training camps in Europe, South Africa and Australia as well as to less glamorous resorts such as Boston in Lincolnshire, and Holme-pierrepoint National Watersports Centre at Nottingham – but this Sisyphean routine was strictly adhered to. You never got more than two days off, except at Christmas, unless you were Cracknell, the picture of rower dedication, who trained on Christmas morning too. None of the crew had a job. The days of the solicitor, the industrialist, the teacher and the chef were long gone. These were crack professionals.

Although the long hours' ploughing lonely furrows in the water were potentially dull, one gradually began to find a grim satisfaction in the hypnotising effect of routine, combined with the curious grip that rowing can have on one. Rowing has an infuriating habit of revealing one's frailties. Yet many who take up the sport find that they cannot resist the urge to try to improve their style, however many times and in however many ways they get it wrong, and despite knowing perfection is impossible.

Much of the work was low-intensity and undertaken below the aerobic threshold, very unlike many people's idea of jumping around in gyms, running and sitting on bicycle machines. The crew did not – excepting Cracknell – race each other all the time. It was more a matter of sawing away at an ergometer for ninety minutes or doing repetition training in the gym. The idea was to speed up the delivery of oxygen to the muscles by expanding the blood capillaries. This was achieved by working to predetermined pulse rates.

Grobler might ask the crew to row ten 2 kilometre pieces at 'UT2', indicating a heartbeat of between 135 and 155 beats a minute. The next level up would be five 2 kilometre pieces at 'UT1', meaning a pulse rate of 155 to 165 beats a minute. At this point the oarsman is standing at the anaerobic threshold, where the body's demand for oxygen matches its maximum ability to take up oxygen. Hearts pound away at about 175 beats a minute. That hurts. The crew could linger here between fifteen and twenty minutes, before it became too painful. Over the threshold, your muscles use more oxygen than the body can absorb, and you step into a land of oxygen debt, nausea and blackouts. You're sprinting, but slowing down all the time, with your heart about to explode at up to 180 beats a minute. The crew would do very little work at this intensity.

Grobler's programme was designed to bring you to the physical edge without tipping you over it. He knew he couldn't expect 100 per cent all the time, or the crew would burn out. He would never ask anyone to lift a weight or put in an ergo score that was beyond them. Had he done so, people would have suffered. The programme differed greatly from that of twenty years earlier, when the squad of time-starved amateurs gave it an hour and a half every evening in the gym, blasting away at sprints and speed circuits undertaken in oxygen debt, while racing each other and the clock. In comparison, Grobler's way was a long, slow measured burn.

To fuel the body, each crew member consumed between 6000 and 7000 calories each day, about three times the average intake for an adult. Oarsmen didn't eat as much as they liked; they ate as much as they could. Every morning at 6 a.m., Foster's Goblin teasmade would make him two cups of tea: one to help him get out of bed, the other for the drive from Oxford, where he lived. Before leaving the house, he'd empty the contents of his breadmaker, where hopefully there would be a sultana loaf that he'd remembered to make the night before. After his first training session at Leander he'd wolf breakfast: five Weetabix, and a whole can of baked beans and several poached eggs on six slices of toast. After the second training session he had lunch: pasta with a cheesy sauce. Arriving home, he'd have toasted pancakes and more tea. Dinner would be based on rice or potatoes. Every dish would be three times larger than you'd expect to find at a 'normal' dinner table. Foster brought his own special bowl to hold the mountain of pasta he ate at lunch. One oarsman ate out of a dog bowl. Others might use flowerpots.

En route to a training camp in Sydney, the squad stopped over for a night in Kuala Lumpur. The majority of the squad headed off to dine at McDonald's. Redgrave, Foster and fellow squad members Ed Coode and Dot Blackie decided to eat native. They truffled out a suitably low-key looking Malaysian restaurant. The menu was written in both Malay and very poor English. It wasn't clear what exactly each dish was so they blindly ordered what they thought was a reasonable selection. They knew they'd got it wrong when the restaurateur began drawing up several tables alongside their own. A huge succession of Malaysian delicacies followed. Coode drew the short straw. He ended up with just a bowl of porridge with a whole fish laid across the top of it.

During the long periods spent abroad, Foster found himself craving simple dietary pleasures like English sausages and tea. By the time the Barcelona Olympics had ended, he'd already spent several weeks abroad on training camps. After

Barcelona he took a month off in Morocco. Returning home via Spain, he noticed a sign saying 'McDonalds 500m' and found himself *running* towards the golden arches.

The nature of the crew's quest and the Redgrave five-gold-medals 'story' opened rowing up to a wider, more clueless audience than ever before. The media greeted the crew's masochistic rites with a mix of admiration, bewilderment and a furtive temple-tapping apprehension that international oarsmen were one step away from being wacko-the-diddlyo.

'Most international rowers are loonies,' wrote Simon Hughes in the *Daily Telegraph*. 'There is no better way to categorise people who get up before some of us have gone to bed, flog up and down the river in horrible weather, pushing their heart rate to inhumane levels, then hasten to the gym to put themselves through the sort of physical punishment found only in Chinese water torture chambers ... then back on the water for another hour of low paid masochism.'

Bethan Bell, Foster's girlfriend, gave an insight into how the domestic fringe coped with the oarsman's workload. 'Tim would leave each morning at 6 a.m. and be back by 5 p.m. with just enough energy to put on his video of the 1981 FA Cup Final,' she wrote in *The Times*. 'Our house is full of drying rowing kit like Lycra stalactites hanging from the banisters and over the tops of doors.' Other than Pinsent's library, the closest most of the squad ever got to cultural nourishment was yoghurt. One evening Bell dragged Foster to *Turandot*. 'With a fine but unwitting sense of ironic timing, Tim's snores gently reverberated to "Nessun Dorma" ... Tiredness makes Tim peculiar. He waits until he is exhausted before stubbornly resisting my pleas and embarks on sorting out the garden shed in the dark, or tidying up his old university notes in the spare room, just to prove that he can. This makes me frustrated, which makes him grumpy and we finally go to bed dreading the sound of the alarm that seems to allow us less sleep every morning.'

One day Foster and Bell went on a 'touristy' day out in London, taking in The Planetarium and Madame Tussaud's. When the lights came on after a video presentation at The Planetarium, Bell turned to Foster to say, 'Wasn't that great?', to find Foster fast asleep.

Journalists and television crews beat an increasingly worn path to the Leander Club. Redgrave didn't mind giving interviews, so long as they didn't interfere with training. Every journalist was therefore treated to the spectacle of Redgrave chomping his way through an Everest of bread and strawberry jam, and Pinsent hosing down litres of orange squash in between training sessions.

'Why not take it easier with the Games so far off?' one journalist asked Redgrave.

'Today is always the most important day,' he smouldered. 'You can never get it back. What you do today is money in the bank. If you don't do it, then it's a day's loss of earnings. When the time comes for repayment, it won't be there if you don't put in the work now.'

'What if you miss one session?'

'If you miss one session, then why not miss another one? It's easier to get a routine, and it makes life easier if you stick to training hard every day.'

In interviews, Redgrave was a rare superstar who came across pretty much as advertised – a very straightforward, fundamentally good bloke. If he sometimes came across as intimidating, it was only the intimidating that four gold medals can't help being. Otherwise, the press actually found him quite hard to spin. Although his currency was gold medals, everything about Redgrave was understated. He didn't do flashy. While younger squad oarsmen proudly flaunted the official kit, Redgrave was never happier than wearing his oldest flip-flops and most ripped pair of rowing shorts, preferably a particular black embroidered pair he'd picked up from the World Championships on Lake Karapiro in New Zealand in 1978. They were comfortable, conspicuously unostentatious, and not quite Harvest Festival. Whenever he sat in an armchair, his crew-mates had to check he wasn't displaying more of his medal-winning class than necessary. After the Sydney Olympics, he was given a flashy watch, which he felt compelled to wear out of politeness. It was heavier than a full cup of coffee and so un-Steve. For a sports star in the same pantheon as Spitz and Lewis, he was extraordinarily ordinary, uncomplicated yet unfathomable, a beguiling mix of self-confidence and modesty, a true sporting hero who was unsentimental about his sport, yet consumed by it.

'People have a preconceived idea of sportsmen,' says Foster. 'They think Steve is cast in the superhuman single-minded potential five-times-Olympic-gold-medallist mould, a riddle wrapped in a mystery inside an enigma. They don't see him as a normal person.'

Some elements of the press weren't happy with this portrayal of the crew as a normal bunch of lads. The media wanted tales of epic purpose and sporting valour. They also wanted spin-off stories of the 'other two' starry-eyed youngsters – Cracknell and Foster – rowing with their hero. They wanted Cracknell and Foster to admit that they and Pinsent would step into their boat each morning and push it out into the middle of the river, whereupon Redgrave would walk out to join them. Some interviews took on an almost Monty Pythonesque surrealism.

A journalist from a broadsheet newspaper with esteemed sports pages serenaded Cracknell and Foster at Caffe Uno in Henley.

'So, Steve's your god, isn't he,' she stated, no question mark in her tone.

'Well, we wouldn't call him a god exactly, but he's a fantastic oarsman. In fact, one of the nice things about Steve is that he's such a normal pers—'

'Yes, but what's it like rowing next to your god?'

'Well ... He's not a god to us. You see, Steve has got to where he is by sheer dedication. Without that dedication, he's like anyone else. That's why we have such respect for him.'

'Yes, but he *is* the messiah, isn't he?'

'... No, he's not the messiah. He's just a naughty boy.'

Even from the start, the crew had the impression that the media desperately wanted them to succeed and nicknamed them the 'Fab Four'. The majority of the rowing press are ex-oarsmen ever-ready to come onside and bring home a good story. Even when Redgrave and Pinsent treated them with disdain, they still hailed them as heroes. As for the four, even the non-rowing press was trumpeting them as a great success story before they had even had one outing.

One interview at the Leander Club jolted Redgrave and Pinsent out of their feathered beds. In a hastily thrown-together appointment with the journalist Joanna Coles, the two oarsmen came across as rude and difficult. Pinsent was lost in a magazine; Redgrave was monosyllabic. They seemed to make 'insider' jokes at Ms Coles's expense. ('Knowing her, I'd have been rude too,' one rowing journalist muttered. 'It wasn't a match made in heaven.') She wrote it how it was. Shocked, Redgrave and Pinsent realised what an easy ride the rowing press had given them. They twigged that part of being a professional sportsman involved 'putting out' and that, far from disdaining and despising the print media, they actually needed it. From then on, Redgrave was more co-operative; Pinsent was still superior, but at least polite.

Although Redgrave was 'the story', he deliberately tried to shun the limelight unless his crew-mates were alongside. Whenever photographers requested pictures of Redgrave alone, he allowed one shot, then insisted the others join in, especially Pinsent. Whenever the crew lined up for a group shot, Redgrave made sure that Foster or Cracknell or both were positioned between himself and Pinsent to prevent picture editors cropping out 'the other two'. He strove to avoid giving the impression that this was his benefit season and that he was carrying on for the limelight. He felt it was Pinsent's 'turn'. Asked about being the 'best in the world', he denied it and produced Pinsent as the best in a deliberate handing over of the torch.

'I'm embarrassed by it all,' he said before the 1999 World Championships. 'I don't get trapped by my reputation. I don't get sucked in by what others think of me. You achieve what you achieve. If others respect you for it, great. But those names they give you, all those silly titles ... They voted me Sportsman of the Decade, or some such thing the other day, and all I could think was, "What about Matthew?" He has done exactly the same as me in the 1990s and not got a fraction of the recognition.'

At press conferences, journalists only ever wanted to talk to Steve, leaving the others to twiddle their thumbs. 'Don't forget Matthew was going for his third gold medal,' said Foster. 'Imagine if Matthew were Linford Christie. He was the second most successful Olympian in God knows how long, yet he just gets forgotten about.'

To remind the media that there were three other oarsmen in the four, it was decided the crew would field questions by rota. When it came to Cracknell's turn, he stayed silent. The others would leap into the void, and so a three-man loop developed. For the first two years, Cracknell's knotted silence was only untied if he was fired direct questions such as, 'James, what did you eat for breakfast?' When the press finally got round to asking the 'other two' questions, the first question was invariably: 'How do you feel about being an equal part of the four but getting so little attention and a fraction of the cash?'

Not that press coverage made much difference. They could be gods in the Leander Club or to their peers, but if they trod more than a few feet outside the Leander Club into the civilian world they were just a group of weird nobodies with pumped-up bodies who couldn't cross their legs. While the crew slogged up and down the river, the rest of Henley, from dog-walkers to ducks, remained happily oblivious to the local legends at work. Foster was once recognised by a member of the public – but only in his opticians, so that didn't count. Only in the Olympic year would strollers hail them.

The crew had tremendous presence within the rowing world, however. Henley Reach practically became their private property. Crews from neighbouring boat clubs, Henley Rowing Club and Upper Thames, fled for the bank as the four surged past. In one incident, the four nearly collided head-on with a veteran crew from Henley Rowing Club. It was as much Lean-der's fault as Henley's. Henley were so mortified that after-wards they went round to Leander to apologise in person. Training at Putney on the Thames just before the Head of the River race in March 1998, the crew, then rowing as part of a national squad eight put together especially for the Head, paddled past the Putney boathouses. Ordinarily, a national squad eight would attract furtive glances from the 'hard'. When this eight went past, people tapped each other on the shoulder and openly gawped.

Grobler was more trainer than technical coach. One of the curious things about rowing is that it is very hard to tell what exactly makes a boat go faster. If you strip away factors such as boat design and weather, and focus on the crew, the variables to juggle are power, weight, height and technique, technique being the killer. However 'scientific' one's approach to rowing, it is extremely difficult to analyse how and when an oarsman's power is most usefully applied in order to produce pace. Many decades ago, a learned professor was even ready to prove that, under the accepted rules of dynamics, the conventional movements of a crew in a rowing boat ought by rights to make it go backwards.

Grobler's approach to coaching rowing technique was: if it ain't broken, don't fix it. Some coaches look at what your little finger is doing on the oar handle or the movement of your outside shoulder. Grobler concentrated on the movement of the boat, but forgave individual defects, such as Pinsent leaning into his rigger. He would say very little during outings. Out on the river, he might utter one prized word, such as 'Acceleration'. Quite often, you might not notice him at all, then suddenly he'd pop out from behind a bush with a stopwatch. Trainee coaches would turn up at Leander and follow him along the towpath to learn from him, then complain that he didn't say anything.

Technical coaching was Foster's domain. 'I may be the runt of the litter,' he said, 'but if there is a technical flaw, I'll spot it. It's not just getting the miles done, but getting them done well. If I go on the water and row 20 kilometres, I make sure each kilometre is as good as I can possibly make it. I'm not going to go out *just to complete 20 kilometres*.'

As the crew paddled along, Foster would chatter away... 'Push the power curve earlier' ... 'Quicker on to the power-peak' ... 'Flowing hands' ... '0.1 of a second quicker lifting hands at the catch' ... 'Reach for the water a further three inches' ... The crew was not always a pretty sight. Each crew member had his stylistic faults. Pinsent tended to shorten up. Foster flexed his arms too early in the stroke. Redgrave appeared to kick with his legs long before the rest of his body had twigged what was going on. Cracknell's finish was suspect. One of the crew's main faults was a tendency to be back-ended, meaning they tended to be lazy at the catch and in the middle (and most effective) part of the stroke, but compensate for it by giving the oar a great tug at the finish.

The others knew Foster's commentary was not intended to destroy their rowing. His words were taken as positively critical. He never shouted, 'Row like me!' Cracknell, on the other hand, would often come across as negative in his criticism. In fact Redgrave once said, 'I've never met anyone more positive than Tim, nor anyone as negative as James.'

During the first few months of the four's existence, the seating order of the crew was shuffled and reshuffled several times before the final line-up was established. With their punchy, brutal strokes, Pinsent and Redgrave tended to bully the other two technically, so it was decided to split them up by putting Pinsent at stroke, Foster at 3, Redgrave at 2 and Cracknell at bow.

Without hard data, you could never be sure what made a boat go faster, or even if it were going faster at all. A numbers man – and a master of arcane calculations about wind speed against the performance of a crew – Grobler focused on improving 'measurables': physiology, boat speed, ergometer times and physical strength. Boat speed over 2000 metres was the most important measurable, but that should improve as other measurables improve. New ideas were introduced one at a time, and their effect measured if possible. His crews never improvised in public and avoided quick fixes, as these tended to crack up in a race. Grobler trained the crew hard during the winter to improve physiology, which if nothing else instilled confidence that they had done the work and 'deserved' to win. Other Groblerisms were: always go out to win; keep a bottomless tool box; and check everything one more time.

He was the most professional person the crew had ever met. When he arrived in England in 1991, British rowing was coached by enthusiastic amateurs who like as not were schoolteachers. Grobler was surprised by how primitive and amateurish British rowing was. 'Conditions were a lot worse than in the GDR,' he said. 'When I came over, I couldn't really understand that we had to go out and find the money to go to the World Championships. To carry the British flag for the country, people have to pay for it! A big shock for me.'

In 1993, he took the squad to Grünau Regatta in East Berlin, ostensibly to compete but in reality to show them the facilities and the way rowing there was treated as a profession. 'There was one building for physiologists,' says Foster, 'and another for doctors and the bio-feedback boat [which simulates the rowing stroke even more faithfully than an ergometer machine] which had strain gauges and a computerised feed-back. The rowing course had floating pontoons every 250 metres on which stood cameras so that the coach could monitor the crews. Having been given an image of Eastern Europe as downtrodden, we were amazed at how rosy life was for an athlete. They had fantastic facilities.'

A master puppeteer, Grobler was a shrewd assessor of situations and a wily manipulator of talent. He would project different personas depending on who he was dealing with or what the occasion demanded. To the general public, he played the absolute dedicated professional. When coaching, he might come across as vague and even disorganised. One morning, he might not appear to have a training programme in mind at all.

This was part of a deeper game played with an element of stage management. He was forever tweaking the atmosphere in which training was conducted, subtly to alter the mood of the crew. Some days were meant to be mentally and physically tough; others were more relaxed.

He was an entirely different coach to each crew member, and read them like books. Grobler knew Cracknell was a worrier and a frustrated perfectionist prone to supererogatory training. He'd adopt a paternal, sympathetic stance and tried to keep things simple for James by setting specific targets and telling him not to strive after more than one goal at the same time. With Foster, he played the frustrated technical coach. With Pinsent, he would be cajoling, and if necessary would man the cattle prods ... Pinsent was almost uncoachable because he won all Grobler's most cherished land-training tests.

'We work very well together,' says Foster. 'I like Jürgen and I think he likes me. I'm different to Matthew and Steve. He told me he considers me mentally very tough. I cope well with pressure. Others might say I'm too stupid to notice. I can do the training very professionally and to a high quality, but with a smile on my face.'

With Redgrave, Grobler would come on the hard task-master. He and Redgrave fed off one another. At training camp in Australia, Redgrave asked to take a day off to organise a Supersprint rowing event. Grobler was unhappy. Training camp was, after all, sacrosanct. After a terse exchange, Grobler released Redgrave. Later, without telling Grobler, Redgrave demolished 20 kilometres on the ergometer machine just to prove he wasn't shirking training.

Redgrave later told the crew what he'd done, but had no need to inform Grobler. Jürgen was psychic, telepathic, had eyes in the back of his head and a sixth sense when keeping tabs on his charges. On one occasion, the crew visited the New South Wales Academy of Sport in Narrabeen, north of Sydney. They met Harald Jahrling, head coach of the Australian national squad, who had won two Olympic gold medals under Grobler. Chatting with the crew, Jahrling reminisced about how funny it had been to row off around the corner of the river out of sight, hide for an hour, then time their re-emergence as if they had completed the full distance.

'Ho-ho-ho, und Jürgen never knew nothing about it,' chortled Jahrling.

That evening, Grobler joined them for dinner. '*Also*, Harald,' he said, 'you remember when you used to hide behind the corner and you thought I never knew. Ha-ha-ha!'

For twenty years, Jahrling had thought he'd got away with it, whereas Grobler had factored their shirking into the programme.

Each summer, the squad would go altitude training at Silvretta, 2000 metres above sea level in the Austrian Alps, above Galtür. On one occasion, the crew was rowing 20 kilometres. Mountain winds and rough conditions meant they weren't able to use the full 2 kilometre course. After 18 kilometres, Redgrave and Pinsent had had enough. Wind and waves were making the boat almost unrowable. Cracknell, however, insisted on carrying on. Foster, in charge of quality control, brokered a deal.

'If we reach the 500 metre mark having achieved a clean release of the blade more than once every two strokes, we'll go home,' he said. 'Instead of covering the full 20 kilometres, we'll have rowed 19.'

He had a deal. Once the crew had been set a task like that, it was amazing how easily they could stick to it. Pinsent's blade, having dragged messily from the water, began to exit as cleanly as you like. Satisfied with the day's work done, 19 kilometres under their belts and money in the bank, the crew paddled home. Grobler, who had been coaching from a vantage point up a hill, wasn't to be seen. When the crew eventually found him, his expression matched the weather.

'So they're going to shorten the rowing course at Sydney, are they, huh?' he seethed. 'Eh? You think they will reduce the distance? You didn't complete the distance.'

The crew slunk off and rowed 1000 metres on the ergometer.

4

Money, or Lack of It

For all his protestations of Pinsent's superiority and disavowals of greatness, Redgrave took the lion's share of the £1m sponsorship that he and Pinsent received from Lombard. 'It's never bothered me,' said Pinsent when asked. 'I don't row because of the fame and the attention; that's a nice add-on. Financially I've attracted much more money in rowing than I could have without Steve. I'm the best-paid rower in history apart from Steve.'

Traditionally, representing your country at international rowing was an expensive pastime. In order to take part in the 1994 and 1995 World Championships, each oarsman in the British squad had to fork out £1500. Foster was one of the lucky ones. He was funded by the Sports Aid Foundation, which helped out the top 100 British Olympic athletes to the tune of £14,000 a year each, which, in Foster's case, the ARA distributed. The breakdown of where the money went was roughly: £3000 for living expenses, £2500 for capital items such as ergometers and equipment and £3000 for training expenses, while the balance went to fund training camps. It wasn't much, but it allowed Foster to train full-time. Cracknell wasn't so lucky. Until 1996 he wasn't one of the chosen few, and received half Foster's amount. Consequently he had had to take part-time jobs, bouncing and working at a bar.

There was an art to submitting your funding application. You applied for what, ideally, you needed in annual expenses. Some athletes went about this more shrewdly than others. The man who said that he could move back to his parents' home and get them to pay for food was awarded a grant of £200 for a pair of trainers. If you were already earning money within your sport – as were Pinsent and Redgrave, thanks to sponsorship – then you didn't qualify for cash handouts at all.

Even in the 'Fab Four', Foster and Cracknell scraped by. They earned in one year what a middle-ranking Premiership footballer earned in one week: £16,500 paid jointly by the Lottery and by Lombard Finance.

Redgrave and Pinsent's original sponsorship deal had not provided for any other oarsmen they might find themselves rowing with. After Athole Still, acting for Redgrave and Pinsent, had secured a million-pound deal from Lombard, David Tanner, the Great Britain international rowing manager, signed the contract gleeful at big figures rolling in. Barely had the ink dried on all those noughts when Cracknell and Foster joined forces with Pinsent and Redgrave. Yet the deal failed to relate to them, except that they were obliged to wear Lombard-branded clothing.

'The deal up to that point seemed to be run on a goodwill basis,' says Foster. 'At first James and I played the game. Then we had an eyes-widening occasion when we asked ourselves, "Hey, what if we each get personal sponsorship from, say, Lombard's biggest competitor?" We didn't exactly start lighting braziers or working to rule, but, since my money came from the National Lottery Foundation, I wore an NLF cap and would make a point of arriving at appointments even later than usual, claiming my 160,000 mile Vauxhall Cavalier had failed to leave on time.'

Lombard saw what was up, and leased Foster and Cracknell a car each. Eventually, in late 1998, Foster and Cracknell signed a deal with Lombard. The following year they each received £3000 from Lombard. 'Whether that money came from Steve and Matthew's pocket, I don't know,' says Foster. 'I don't know how much Steve and Matthew got from Lombard. Athole Still would have taken their cut. During the Olympic year, James and I received £10,000 each from Lombard, which was great. It was a small percentage but of a large cake. We were poor relations, but nonetheless grateful ones.'

5

1997: The Dream Start

The four made its competitive debut at the World Cup regatta at Munich in May 1997. Munich is a man-made course originally built for the Munich Olympics in 1976. Located some distance from the city, it is renowned for its 20,000 seater grandstand, sparkling clear waters and giant fish. After bleak winter mornings ploughing up and down the river in private, the first regatta of the season is time to break out of the chrysalis. It is a meeting place, proving ground and arena for display both on and off the water. Redgrave drew attention, but never flaunted his presence. Neither he nor Pinsent had time for convivial loiterings, which added to their serious businesslike image and made them seem somehow above it all, and harder to beat.

Redgrave was accorded a status normally reserved for single scullers. The only comparable figure in the sport was Perti Karpinnen, the Flying Finn and triple Olympic gold-medal-winning single sculler, who had long since retired. Redgrave was the real thing: a living, rowing god. His sheer size made him stand out. A Romanian rower nudged Cracknell at one regatta.

'How heavy is he?' he whispered, pointing to Redgrave.

Cracknell replied with a suitably heavily stacked muscular number, throwing in a few extra kilograms for effect.

'Oh, he's so strong,' swooned the Romanian. 'I am so weak.'

Many rowers work at their physique, but Redgrave had it naturally in the form of huge bolt-on muscles on his legs, arms and shoulders. Pinsent had it naturally too. His frame was even larger than Redgrave's but less startlingly muscle-bound and less developed. Were you seated behind Pinsent in a boat, his back loomed like a side of beef. Pinsent's official weight was 108 kilograms, but at times it would balloon to 115 kilograms. By comparison, Foster and Cracknell looked puny.

Redgrave's approach to competition was: frighten the hell out of the opposition and don't let them believe they stand a chance. Reduce them to dispirited galley slaves. In Redgrave's mind, this softening-up process had begun months earlier. During trials in March 1997, he was pondering that opening Munich salvo. 'When we get there in May,' he said, 'we need to send out a big message.'

Typical race tactics were to go off hard, establish a lead, sit back and enjoy the battle for minor placings being thrashed out in one's wake. Above all, try to make it look easy. After each victorious race, while the opposition slumped gasping for air, the four would rub it in by 'casually' paddling off as if they'd hardly had to try. They cultivated the mystique of an 'extra' unused gear. The British crew didn't want merely to be unbeaten, they wanted to be unbeatable too.

Truth or fiction? The Poles certainly believed it. They came up against the British four in every heat of every international regatta that year. They tried everything to squeeze past Great Britain, but were easy fodder. Rival crews fell for the air of British invincibility too. An air of resignation hung about them. The Germans even waved at the British four during warm-ups. 'We know we've got them beaten every time,' said Cracknell. Even the Italians, a perceived threat, 'seemed a little too happy', said Crackell, and acted as if they'd won when they finished second.

Foster was above – or beneath – mind games. He avoided them, and preferred to fraternise with opponents than try to psych them out. 'Having raced against someone, I felt I had a bond with them that I wanted to share,' he said.

The crew won comfortably at the Munich regatta, and won again a few weeks later at the Paris international regatta held in an adapted part of a lake near Disneyland. Everything was going to plan. The only disappointment was the absence of the Oarsome Foursome, who were taking an extended time out.

Sunday, 6 July 1997

At Henley Royal Regatta in 1997, the four, rowing as Leander Club & Oxford University ('Oxford University' referring to Foster), entered the Stewards' Challenge Cup for international standard coxless fours. No other crew had entered, until at the eleventh hour, Nottinghamshire County Rowing Association submitted a speculative entry of two lightweight pairs cobbled together.

Leander decided to have fun. Blasting off at a mad rate, they tried to break the Barrier record of 1 minute 51 seconds. They failed, but passed the Barrier with a comfortable lead. Pinsent took the rate down from 44 to 18 strokes a minute. The crew paddled 'light'.

Redgrave asked how everyone was feeling. 'Let them come back at us,' he said.

Nottinghamshire began catching up. As the commentator, who at Henley merely gives the rating (strokes per minute) of each crew and the distance between each crew at various points along the course, called the race, it appeared that this scratch, no-hope, lightweight outfit were eating up the river, while Leander had all but stopped rowing. Passing the enclosures, the commentator boomed, 'THE CREWS ARE LEVEL, NOTTS COUNTY AT 38, LEANDER AT 18!' A hush descended. What was wrong? Then came: 'NOTTINGHAMSHIRE HAVE TAKEN A SLIGHT LEAD!'

'We went from 18 strokes a minute to 52 strokes a minute within three strokes,' says Foster. 'Between the grandstands and the Finish – about 200 yards – we scored an "easy" verdict of more than five boat lengths. I knew the Notts County guys and we had a laugh afterwards. But from the roar of the crowd, there was a sense of relief. It was the first time I'd ever really heard the commentary and the crowd at Henley. Normally, by that stage of the race, your blood has rushed to your muscles, your senses have closed down and you aren't fully aware of your surroundings.'

31 August to 8 September 1997

The World Championships in Aiguebelette spanned the death and funeral of Diana, Princess of Wales. She died on the morning of the four's opening heat, and was buried on the day of their final. 'As the week went on, the situation got worse and worse,' Redgrave told the press. 'It became almost unbearable to watch the pictures on television as the crowd watched her coffin leaving St James's Palace. It was so moving.'

In fact the crew felt totally removed from the Diana drama and sensed nothing of the mass hysteria that gripped Britain. Cracknell, who couldn't have cared less, mulled over the matter in front of his 'Gold Fever' video camera while lying in the bath and reckoned the whole thing was a hysterical overreaction. Then the crew began to be confronted by people pointedly saying, 'Well, obviously you won't be racing then, will you!' It was clear that the four, led by Redgrave, would have to make some sort of lofty, statesmanlike gesture to Diana's obsequies; but it was equally clear that they would race. No question of juddering to a halt, going to pieces and cancelling everything, as had happened that week in Britain. Domestic sporting fixtures could be rescheduled; World Championships could not. Besides, sponsorship contracts were at stake. Still, something had to be done.

The minute's silence that was due to be observed in Britain clashed with the four's warm-up plans for their final. Nevertheless, vests trimmed with black ribbons, the crew warmed up on the sparkling waters of Lac d'Aiguebelette, and then, twenty minutes before their race, held a minute's silence at exactly the same time as in Britain. As they sat there motionless in their boat, a race went off down the course. Philistines! How disgusting of them not to observe the silence!

The British four continued with their warm-up. Then, just to be annoying, ten minutes later the French organisers of the regatta held their own 'official' regatta minute's silence. The crew wondered if they should join in and thereby observe two one-minute's silences. In the end they didn't.

They won their final with a stupendous row that Redgrave downplayed as 'relatively perfect'. They saw off the French, silver-medallists at Atlanta, by nearly four seconds, and comfortably beat Italy, World Champions in 1994 and 1995. They even kept their huge finishing burn under wraps. The 'poetry of their motion on the flat azure waters of Lac d'Aiguebelette at the foot of the Alps in Savoy had the inspiration of Wordsworth about it', wrote Nick Townsend in the *Daily Mail*.

Less poetic during the race was Redgrave himself. He wouldn't shut up. He kept shouting encouragement at the crew. When he cried, 'This one's for the Australians,' Foster looked around for a seventh crew and thought, *Hang on, the Australians aren't in this race. They're having a year off.*

Redgrave wanted to rub home a message to the Australians, who were absent but plotting a four for Sydney.

As they got out of their boat, Foster and Cracknell hugged each other. They'd won their first senior World Championship titles, and had proved a point to themselves as well as to Redgrave and Pinsent.

Several other British medallists received their prizes and burst into tears. The four, however, disdaining excitability and emotional volatility as poor rostrum etiquette, bowed their heads in unison as the Union flag rose to half-mast. 'We just wanted to show our respects, just as everyone back home was showing theirs, for Princess Diana,' said Redgrave, who tucked his medal into his vest for the national anthem. 'There were times when it was difficult to keep your mind on what we had come here for, but we had talked through a plan and there was a grim determination that we would fulfil it.'

As the strains of 'God Save the Queen' died, the large contingent of British fans applauded. Redgrave looked at the Union flag and quietly crossed himself, almost touching the black ribbon on his chest as he did. 'What we have achieved here doesn't mean much in life's journey,' he said, 'but life must go on. I just hope the marks of respect we made show that we felt exactly the same as everyone back home.'

Back in Britain, the four were elevated to national heroes, not just for winning in style, but for their adroit handling of the Diana situation. The sight of the crew, lined up four abreast on the pontoon, in their kit, bare-footed, heads down, listening to the national anthem, arms behind their backs in identical poses, like four balloon-chested statues from the same mould, was the enduring image of the championships and was blazed across the Sunday press. It summed up the crew: sticking to the job but understatedly and respectfully. The four were portrayed as patriotic warriors stranded in a distant land with no choice but to fight on. To the media, the proper emotion, the seemly sentiment, the fitting moral tone, and of course the right sporting result, were seen to prevail. There was even talk of the enrichment of the Redgrave legend.

The following Monday, the legend of Grobler's timekeeping cracked. The crew were dreading their 8 a.m. flight home, but were highly amused when Grobler overslept and missed it. He was livid. Never once in thirty years of coaching had he ever missed a flight. The bear growled furiously at the wasp. From then on, whenever Grobler said, 'You must be ready at such-and-such a time,' the temptation was to think, 'Oh well, that's just Jürgen time.'

Throughout the whole of that first year-long quarter-turn of the Olympic wheel, the four wiped the floor with the field. They won every race at the Munich, Paris and Lucerne inter-national regattas. Not even further protests from Redgrave's body – chest and throat infections and stomach bugs galore – could halt the four's relentless advance.

Foster knew that everything he'd heard and read about Redgrave and Pinsent was an understatement. 'Whatever people say about Steve and Matthew, they really are quite good,' he commented after their first win at Munich. 'Pre-viously I'd raced hoping to win. This crew expects to win.'

6

1997–8: Oh Sugar!

After a light outing at Henley just after the traditional autumn break, Redgrave felt a raging thirst. 'I drank a pint of water, and still felt thirsty. I drank another pint of water, and still felt thirsty. After three or four pints of fluid and still feeling this tremendous thirst, I thought, *Hmmm, I know what this is, I've had it before*.'

He tested the sugar level in his urine with a dipstick. His blood-sugar levels were off the scale. He rang his GP. 'My immediate reaction was, "I've finally pushed my body over the edge. Well, it's been a pretty good innings. Time to stop." ' This train of thought lasted as long as it took to drive from his GP's practice to Wycombe General Hospital.

Redgrave claims he had symptoms of diabetes in 1993 as a direct result of the colitis he had had before the Barcelona Olympics in 1992; colitis is a pre-cancerous condition for which Redgrave has to take continual medication, even when he has no symptoms.

Diabetes proved more of a problem than Redgrave let on. At first, it was openly discussed by crew and media. Other examples of diabetic sportsmen were dug out and held up, such as Gary Mabbut, who played football for Tottenham

Hotspur. Mabbut was hardly comparable; football is no endurance sport, not even at Spurs.

Redgrave knew the risks he was taking. Diabetes is a debilitating, unpredictable illness that can be treated by injections of insulin. A side effect of training with insulin in your blood is plummeting blood-sugar levels, which can induce a diabetic coma. To begin with, Redgrave radically changed his diet, and cut out a lot of sugar; but it didn't seem to work: he kept running out of energy. Resuming training was agony, physically and mentally. In circuit training, he had to force himself to finish, but still underperformed. He felt himself falling short of superhumanity. He experienced the humiliation of fighting not to be the best, or even to compete, but to survive. Previously, he'd competed against other oarsmen; now he was fighting against a potentially less tractable opponent.

One morning in November 1997, Redgrave appeared at Leander wearing a bobble hat. He'd never worn a bobble hat before. The squad was suspicious. What was wrong with him this time? Some senior Leander members, then training for Rentacrew Boat Club (the name of the Leander 'old heavies'), assumed that Redgrave's health had called for some ghastly radiotherapy treatment, and took pity on him. Nothing was wrong. A hair re-growth clinic had approached Redgrave to see if he was interested in a Graham Gooch-style rug. Redgrave had gone along to see what the fuss was about, and had his hair shaved off and a wig fitted. Very few people witnessed the bewigged Redgrave, since the rug only stayed on for as long as it took Redgrave to realise the futility of what he was doing. He removed the bobble hat to howls of laughter from the squad. Redgrave fretted that his children might find him scary. Instead, they took one look at him and called him Mr Potato Head. He was more embarrassed by his momentary lapse into vanity than by the lack of hair. Foster suggested the entire crew shave their heads and call themselves the 'Four Skins'.

Redgrave struck his diabetic nadir on training camp in Cape Town in late 1997. The land-based programme involved 70 mile cycling rides. None of the squad is a natural cyclist, Redgrave least of all. Grobler had found a route that took the squad over rolling hills. They set off as a pack. The speed of the pack is greater than the speed of an individual. Redgrave was that individual. On the very first hill, he straggled and took four and a half hours to complete a three-and-a-half-hour ride. This must momentarily have thrown Cracknell, who took the view that a cycling training session only *began* when the first man cracked and got left behind. For Redgrave to blow up so soon almost spoilt it for him.

By Christmas 1997 Redgrave was so far behind, he had to train alone. Struggling and ill, he absented himself from the Leander Club for days on end. The squad had been training in sculling boats, so it wasn't as if there were three oarsmen waiting for Redgrave to go out in the four. Nonetheless, Grobler and Pinsent felt put out. Grobler admits he considered dropping Redgrave.

That Christmas, doctors collected twelve biopsies of Redgrave's colon at Charing Cross Hospital. 'I suppose that whole period is the closest I've ever been to chucking it all in,' he said. How close was close? 'Out of ten? Nine and three-quarters. I decided I was going to tell Jürgen I'd had enough.'

One week before Christmas, Redgrave rang Foster. It was the last day of official training before Grobler flew home to Germany, leaving the squad to train individually. It was unusual for him to ring. Redgrave and Foster wouldn't necessarily chat over the telephone, but this was a normal, friends-type conversation. Redgrave explained that training wasn't getting him anywhere and that he felt low. Foster agreed that the best thing Redgrave could do was take a break, go away and start afresh in the New Year.

Without telling Grobler, Redgrave slipped away for two weeks' skiing in California. He felt ill and dejected. Preying on his mind was the thought that the doctors feared Crohn's disease, a potentially cancerous condition in which you lose parts of your colon. Why else take so many biopsies? This would have been more serious. Crohn's would have sunk his career there and then.

As he attacked the black runs, he wondered if his body was going downhill in other ways. 'I basically went AWOL,' he said. 'I'd never done that before, and I expected a good bol-locking from Jürgen when I got back.' Absenting oneself for reasons of illness or injury was one thing; indulging in extra-curricular activities while pleading illness or injury was altogether different and Grobler frowned on it. 'I was going a bit mad, to say the least,' admitted Redgrave.

What changed his mind? 'I couldn't give it up. I've come through adversity before, and I wasn't prepared to bow to it now. There's another gold medal to be won yet.'

Pinsent, although inwardly concerned, glossed over the matter to Cracknell by telling him how, six weeks before they won their first gold medal in Barcelona, Redgrave had been in hospital on a drip suffering from colitis.

'That put it all into perspective,' said Cracknell.

'Jürgen was very helpful,' says Pinsent. 'He cut Steve some slack when he needed it, and kicked his arse when it was appropriate. It's not easy telling someone with Steve's repu-tation to shut up and get on with it, but it had to be done.'

Redgrave reverted to his pre-diabetic diet and began taking larger slugs of insulin.

On Redgrave's return, there was no reprimand. Grobler put the entire Great Britain rowing squad through a pairs matrix. The squad raced each other in every combination of pair, and the performances were compared to arrive at an order of boat-moving ability. Redgrave approached the matrix feeling better within himself, but still not confident. He surprised himself by finishing second among bowside oarsmen behind Foster, and fourth overall. That there was clear water between the top four oarsmen – Pinsent, Cracknell, Foster and Redgrave – and the rest of the squad was an even bigger boost.

What emerged was that Redgrave was spiralling downwards in a negative vortex caused by the combined effects of colitis and diabetes. The treatment for colitis aggravated the symptoms of diabetes, while the stress of having diabetes aggravated the symptoms of colitis.

'I had such a bad winter and early spring for no apparent reason,' he told the Mail on Sunday. 'Now I know why. The tablets I was taking for colitis made the diabetes worse. I couldn't keep my blood-sugar levels under control and was existing on my fat deposits. Finally I was running out of glycogen, taken from my muscles. I could get by, but suddenly when I asked more of myself, there was nothing there. I wondered where all my energy had gone.'

He had lost a stone in muscle bulk over the previous winter and was thirty seconds off his usual pace in gym tests. Instead of bench-pressing 120 kilograms, he could barely lift 105 kilograms. He never confessed to his teammates the extent of his self-doubt. The matter of a replacement was never discussed, nor did the crew feel Redgrave didn't deserve his seat, as the pairs matrix proved.

After several months, Redgrave mastered the balance. 'In the first three or four months it was very difficult coming to terms with it and knowing how much insulin to take,' said Redgrave. 'Now I've gone back to the diet I was on beforehand, but I'm taking more insulin to counteract the amount of sugar and glucose I eat.'

Eventually diabetes became, in Redgrave's eyes, a non-issue. While the crew couldn't help noticing him checking his blood sugar, and quietly stabbing his stomach with insulin shots in between training sessions, he grew irritated whenever a fuss was made, especially when anyone had the temerity to suggest his chances of winning gold were thereby lessened.

'It's not an issue,' he said one morning to a reporter, peering over the usual mountain of toast and jam. 'I know others have got their views on it, but for me it's normal business. I'm dealing with it ... Look, if I'd twisted an ankle and couldn't train for a week, would people be making a big deal of it? No, of course not. That's how I see the diabetes. Do you know, I haven't missed any training with it at all. I'm doing fine, I'm keeping up with the others, and I'm not receiving any special treatment.'

The crew only ever mentioned Redgrave's diabetes when, bored, they played 'guess the blood-sugar level'. Redgrave would generally be furthest out. When one race was delayed by an hour, Foster found him scoffing Mars bars to keep up his sugar. Golfing with Pinsent one day, Redgrave found he was unable to count. His sugar level had dropped too low.

'Steve can be Steve one minute, up there, fighting, a champion,' says Foster. 'Ten minutes later he's nowhere. Simple mechanical things become impossible. I'd be standing by with a banana saying, "Do you want this?" It's not because he's gone soft. He's run out of sugar.'

7

Rowing Life vs Real Life

What hardships an oarsman will endure and what sacrifices he will make in order to avoid getting a proper job, never mind aim at an Olympic medal! Training to be an Olympic oarsman is a job times three. It monopolises the diary, regardless of weekends and holidays. It demands prodigious life and career sacrifices and submission to a regime of monastic rigour. And for what? There was a time when rowing with distinction was a ticket to the City, but not any more (although something of an Oxbridge blue boat–City pipeline may still exist). The oarsman must not expect recognition or worldly approval. His work is his recompense. Only in his own peace of mind and self-esteem will he find solace. The purity of the sporting achievement in rowing is what makes it beautifully suited to the Olympic ideal. Money and fame would cheapen it.

Of course, not all the squad were such Sir Galahad-ish purists. Part of the challenge for them was to lead a balanced life while dedicating so much of it to this singular activity. Lottery funding eased the strain that this contradiction entailed. It allowed one to dedicate one's life to rowing and, in effect, made rowing a 'proper' job. Qualifying for a Lottery grant, however, demanded a standard of fitness and competence whose very attainment required considerable dedication. Pre-Atlanta, Cracknell found himself caught in this void. It was felt that one reason he blew it at Atlanta was that, denied a Lottery grant, he'd had to hustle for part-time work on top of (over)training, and consequently weakened his resistance to illness.

Grobler took the view that a 'balanced life' was fine, so long as rowing came first. An unwritten rule, which sprang from his professionalism and love of compartmentalising things, was that private life and rowing life were kept apart. Away from the crew, you could stay up late and raise hell, but you had to be ready to train at eight o'clock the following morning. Not that there was much scope for extracurricular corybantics, not once you'd factored in time spent recovering from training, eating and sleeping. Taken seriously – Olympic-gold-medal-winning seriously – rowing is prophylactic to most forms of pleasurable indulgence.

On training camps, there was even less scope for mischief-making, hence Grobler's partiality to them. They were a surreptitious means of controlling the crew's non-rowing lives. Take the annual three-week altitude camp at Silvretta, a spectacular if desolate spot many miles from the nearest nightclub or casino. A glacier calves off into one side of the lake, opposed by a cliff that soars vertically upwards 1000 metres. A road fringes one end of the lake, which is bordered at the other by a dam. Before the gaze of bewildered hikers holidaying in the Alpine scenery, the entire squad would rock up and proceed to buoy a straight 2000 metre course using ARA buoys stored permanently nearby, then hop into boats and row up and down ten times.

In the thin, chilly Alpine air, you struggled to walk more than 400 metres without your lungs heaving with long draughts, never mind row 20 kilometres. The squad dined in a nearby restaurant. To save breath, they drove there and back. 'Jürgen would devour his dinner in two minutes,' says Foster. 'Watching him eat is like watching someone who is about to have their food swiped from under their eyes. Matthew and Steve would have finished theirs in four minutes, just as I was about to tuck into my starter. Jürgen would then start tapping his watch – not that there was any urgency to go anywhere, stuck up there in the mountains.'

The idea of altitude training is to produce extra red blood cells, which the body uses to transport oxygen from the lungs to the muscles. Back at sea level, its advantage wears off after two to three weeks. Performance may even deteriorate owing to the risk of overtraining, infections and general disruption of training, which at altitude has to be reduced.

'Jürgen likes Silvretta,' says Foster. 'It's isolated. There's nothing there except the icy lake, the glacier, the mountains and these hikers. You can focus on the rowing. When I first went there, all we'd take by way of diversion were a few posters to decorate our rooms. These days the ARA packs a trailerload of paraphernalia for extracurricular boatshed activity, Playstations and videos. In 1994 the trailer was refused entry at the Austrian border because it was so over-loaded with boats, kit and electronics. The final straw was Redgrave and Pinsent's massive trunk of chocolate, which had to be ditched.

'Silvretta was never as boring as we feared,' says Foster. 'But I doubt altitude training helps. We'd go up there for nineteen days and return feeling soul-refreshed and fantastic. But is that because we've been at altitude or because we've trained solidly for nineteen days? It may make a fraction of a second difference; but no physiological studies have con-clusively proved that it works.'

During the *longueurs* at training camps, when the Play-station paled and rewinding the video became a chore, Crack-nell and Foster would beguile the hours by dyeing their hair.

They experimented with several colours – purples, reds, greens as well as straight bleach. Cracknell applied so much bleach that his hair acquired the consistency of straw, so he dyed it black to regain a 'normal' colour, which made him look like a cross between Elvis and Lego man. The media could hardly keep up with Cracknell's hair-*don'ts*, more desperate acts of self-expression than fashion statements.

Back in England, when the crew was let off the leash, Grobler trusted them not to do anything stupid and burn the midnight oil every night; but real life had a habit of intruding and undermining Grobler's two-worlds utopian vision. The division of rowing life from private life meant different things to different crew members.

Hovering somewhere between rowing and private life was 'work', meaning appearances, speaking engagements and golf, which sometimes took the form of pro–celebrity charity tournaments. Redgrave was up to here with work. He was forever in and out of tuxedo and Pringle. His diary was presidential in its complexity, and scheduled to the minute, four weeks in advance. A double Olympic gold-medallist, Pinsent was also in demand, but not as much as Redgrave.

Work had to fit in around training and regattas. But if ad hoc changes to the programme were mooted – say a five-day training camp sprung on the crew by Grobler – Redgrave demanded a month's notice, close consultation with his agenda, and would have to 'get back to you'; Pinsent needed a week's notice; Foster, whose diary was subject to change by the minute, required ten seconds; while Cracknell would already have his bags packed and be ready to go.

Redgrave also had a wife and children to look after. Normally, wedding bells toll the imminent demise of an international oarsman's career. It becomes impossible to fit family life around the demands of rowing, and maybe a job too. One element has to go, and it's usually the rowing. The only other married squad member was Greg Searle, who never recaptured his gold-medal-winning form of Barcelona '92. (In 2003, after Pinsent and Cracknell finished a shocking fourth in the World Championships in Milan, the squad thought of pointing out to Cracknell, by then married to Beverley Turner, television presenter, that the reason he'd lost was that he'd got married – just to see how soon it would take him to get divorced.)

Redgrave not only had a wife, Ann, but also three children, Natalie, Sophie and Zak. A girlfriend was one thing; a wife another. But to juggle marriage, three children and an international rowing career was taking masochism to new heights. A continual tug of war was waged, with either side trying to yank Redgrave towards them. He barely managed to strike a balance. Just before the Olympics, the crew shot a video diary, 'Gold Fever'. In one scene, the newly born Zak Redgrave is being cradled by Steve. Two hours later, he hands Zak back to Ann with the words, 'I'm off training.' You actually see him ringing Cracknell, at Code Amber, to see if he wants to go out in a pair. On the other hand, the squad reckoned the births of Sophie and Zak, in February 1994 and 1998 respectively, were shrewdly timed to give Redgrave an excuse to miss the traditional Boston pairs trial.

One day Redgrave *told* Grobler he wouldn't be able to train for one week because it was half-term. Grobler switched into hard-taskmaster mode. Outrageous! What if everyone in the squad wanted a week off to be with their family whenever there was a holiday? A mock argument would ensue, which Grobler would lose.

'By using this tactic, and releasing Steve, Jürgen knew Steve would earn brownie points with his wife and children,' says Foster. 'He also knew Steve would train while he was away. This tactic would never have worked with Matthew.'

Grobler could either be very understanding or he could put his foot down and effectively say 'No!' That Ann Redgrave was an ex-oarswoman herself and British rowing team doctor (she competed at the Los Angeles Olympics, at the Commonwealth Games and at three World Championships), if anything, eased the pressure. She at least understood her husband's commitment. Grobler appreciated that, and knew that allowances would have to be made.

Dr Redgrave travelled to training camps, and sometimes brought the children too. Girlfriends rarely joined training camps. Wives might be admitted for one day; but wife *and* children was unheard of. The whole point of training camps was to cut loose from the domestic fringe, not bring it with you. Squad members were dragooned in to help babysit the Redgrave brood. At Silvretta in 1993, Ann Redgrave entrusted Natalie Redgrave, 3, to Foster, who was off games with a back injury. While Dr Redgrave ministered to the squad, Foster introduced Natalie to a community of pigs that lived down the mountainside. In late 1996, when the coxless four was being trialled, the squad reckoned that Redgrave had switched from a pair in Atlanta to a four at Sydney purely because he had more children to look after and needed babysitters.

The latitude afforded Redgrave allowed him to watch his children grow up. Still, on training camps he room-shared with Pinsent. Dr Redgrave slept elsewhere. Redgrave would have been grateful for this arrangement in Sydney, where Ann Redgrave room-shared with Louise Kingsley, coach of the single sculler Alison Mowbray. Kingsley awoke one morning to find Dr Redgrave showering and preparing for the day – at twenty-five minutes to one at night, not five minutes past seven in the morning as was planned. Dr Redgrave had read her watch upside down.

The sacrifices that rowing demands put your youth on hold. You live in penury, stay incredibly fit, and inhabit a crepuscular world of hitched lifts, shared bedrooms and scrounged meals. You float free from the ties of normal adult life. Cracknell and

Foster, although in their late twenties, led 'student' lives shorn of family commitments. Redgrave led the most 'normal' life, having a wife, family and house. He was lucky his family indulged his boyish pursuit.

Despite the privations of their chosen career, the four still observed Lent. That year, 1998, Pinsent gave up chocolate. Redgrave and Foster gave up being late: if they were five minutes late one day, they had to turn up five minutes early the following day. Cracknell gave up tomato ketchup, but after one week got withdrawal symptoms and began to show signs of sugar deprivation. Grobler intervened. Ketchup was back on the menu.

Unlike Foster, who enjoyed his food and became something of a cook, Cracknell ate to train and scarcely a mouthful passed his lips without ketchup being involved. A bowlful of food would require a quarter of a bottle of ketchup. The squad even set him taste challenges to see if he could distinguish one brand from another. Heinz usually prevailed. When cooking, his speciality was pasta, tuna and broccoli with lashings of ketchup.

It took more than mere Lent to discourage Foster from enjoying his 'active social life' – so active that rowing didn't necessarily come first at all. He partied hard and could be found of an evening doing 'the four-ounce bicep curl, with either left or right hand and sometimes both'. Alcohol prevents the breakdown of lactic acid, which means you wake up the following morning with exhausted muscles that ache as if they've been through a workout. There was nothing wrong with a pint or two. Three or four could make life difficult the next day, but was acceptable. Five or six was asking for trouble; it could be done but was not recommended. Usually your body told you to stop long before Grobler caught on. Grobler's view on alcohol was that if you turned up the next day capable of training, you could drink what you liked; but never try to outdrink an East German oarsman.

At the beginning of his senior career, Foster paired with Martin Cross, the pre-Redgrave squad stalwart ever since 1979. He and Foster were hailed the 'Sorcerer and his Apprentice'. Cross preached that rowing wasn't just about doing what you were told, and that even if you were told to do something, you shouldn't necessarily do it; and, conversely, that you shouldn't wait to be told to do something before going out and doing it. They were instant soulmates. 'Martin was always leading Tim astray,' recalls Dan Topolski, former Oxford rowing coach. 'Tim is a renegade and natural rebel. He loved being the party boy. He could behave disgracefully all night and row like a dream all morning. Others couldn't keep up. He has fantastic resilience.'

As for rowing, Foster was carefree and thought he could get away with things. He'd ask himself, 'If I go out tonight, will it affect my rowing?' His answer was usually, 'No.' He was also accident-prone. On his 18th birthday, he was knocked out when some friends gave him the bumps. (He was detained in hospital for three days while doctors worried about his low pulse. When he told them that his resting pulse was 34, unusually low even for an oarsman, they sent him home.) He was an accident waiting to happen, and it happened.

One Saturday evening in May 1998, Foster went to a Boat Race party thrown in the University Boat Club at Oxford, where he was then living. To celebrate the occasion, he dyed his hair bright red. That night, with the party aswing, Foster was regaling fellow oarsman Luka Grubor with one of his jokes, when he threw back an arm extravagantly, and shattered a nearby window pane. Had he taken care delicately to extricate his hand, the damage might have been superficial; but he instinctively yanked it back inside.

The first thing Foster noticed was that the girl standing next to him was being sprayed with blood. It took him a second or two to twig that the blood was his own, and jetting – at 34 beats a minute if not more – from a wound in his hand. Mercifully anaesthetised, Foster bloodily staggered to the bathroom to wash his hand, and saw raw bone and tendon gaping at him. Grubor removed his favourite Iggy Pop T-shirt, ripped it up and made a tourniquet, and helped carry Foster out of the boathouse. As the fresh air hit, Foster went light-headed and fell down a flight of stairs. The Oxford University Boathouse stands half a mile from the nearest road, so it took several minutes for Foster, bruised, bloodied and helped by Ms Bell, to reach the ambulance.

Doctors staunched the bleeding and told Foster to wait among the bandaged and plastered Saturday night pub-fight victims in Casualty. Only then did he realise his injury was more than just a stupid scratch that bled a lot. The reper-cussions of the accident began to seep into his befuddled brain like water into the hull of a sinking ship. *What have I done?* he thought. *Have I blown everything, not just for me but for the others?*

Three hours elapsed before the doctors examined him prop-erly. Taking one look at Foster's red shoulder-length hair, they didn't believe him when he said he was a professional sportsman. They had him down as some kind of punk rocker.

He had severed the tendons in his little finger, cut deep into his ring finger, sliced his thumb down to the bone, lacerated the artery and lost two pints of blood. He'd need plastic surgery.

'Great,' he said to Bethan, 'you can have your tits done at the same time.' For Foster to say that to his girlfriend, who had carried him across a field, called an ambulance and waited three hours in Casualty, this wasn't quite the final straw, but their relationship ended one year later.

'How long before I can play the piano?' he asked a doctor.

'Six weeks.'

'That's brilliant. I couldn't play it before.'

His hand in a cast, Foster was released from hospital the following day. He would be off rowing for eight weeks. He rocked up at Leander braced for homilies on squandered talent. The crew reacted in different ways. Cracknell shot him a million megawatt glare of disapproval. James viewed Foster's accident as a traitorous episode of rank irresponsibility. He saw his career, funding, his whole life disappearing downriver. Pinsent, less angry, said, 'We were all quite pissed off when we heard about it. And to be honest, if such an accident was going to happen to anyone, it was likely to be Tim. But there was never a law about how we live our lives outside rowing.' Redgrave appeared the least bothered. The crew could carry on with the next best bowside oarsman.

The crew accepted that Foster enjoyed a drink and had friends, but this was a flagrant breach of purity. He'd overstepped the mark, was unable to row, and had therefore jeopardised the programme. His social life had invaded the crew's area.

'They were particularly annoyed that I hadn't rung them,' says Foster. 'I, in turn, was annoyed they hadn't rung me. The rule seemed to be that if you have an accident and aren't actually dead, then you have to ring the boys rather than they ring you. James definitely ignored me. That surprised me. James, whom I thought would be most understanding, wasn't at all, yet he'd been at the same party earlier on that evening. Nor was James risk-free. In February 1997, he'd totalled his motorbike in Putney.' The incident heightened the sense that Foster was a Cavalier in a boat of Roundheads.

'I felt I'd let the others down,' he says. 'I had apologised to Steve and James and would have preferred it if they'd got really angry, but they didn't. We have a brotherly relationship. It was as if I had broken a trust between us by getting myself injured. All sorts of ridiculous thoughts had gone through my mind when I feared I might be out for the season, even that I might have my hand cut off and replaced with a hook to hold the oar.'

The expected roasting from the press never happened. In the bedazzled media's eyes, Foster was unlucky, not a fool. The halo was slightly askew, but still burning bright. 'They never threw us a nasty question,' says Foster. ' "Is Steve a god?" was about as tough as it got. It wasn't as if they were dragging skeletons out of your cupboard.' If anything, the episode boosted his profile. It showed he had a personality. He was beginning to emerge from the shadows of 'other two-ness'.

The crew trained with Simon Dennis (former St Paul's schoolboy oarsman who rowed in the British eight in 1997) for a week, then tried Luka Grubor, who eventually supplanted Foster. Grubor had rowed with Foster in the Oxford blue boat the year before, and house-shared with Cracknell in Reading. Son of a Yugoslavian basketball international, he had represented Yugoslavia as a junior international oarsman and Croatia as a senior, finishing ninth in the world championships in a coxed four. Redgrave thought that Grubor, being larger than Foster, had potential.

Foster was surprised how quickly the crew shunned him. He would cycle 26 miles from Oxford to Leander, train alone, then cycle home, having been ignored by his 'crew-mates'. Grobler assured Foster that, once healed, he'd be back in. He spun a different story to the four, telling them that if they were fast enough with Grubor, they'd stay as they were. Cracknell was inclined not to want Foster back in at all. Luka Grubor was Cracknell's best friend as well as housemate.

In recuperation, Foster spent two weeks at Lilleshall National Sports Centre, in Shropshire. During an already accident-prone, injury-packed career, he was already well acquainted with the two-mile tree-lined drive and 100 acre grounds of this former country retreat and hunting lodge of the Duke of Sutherland, converted into a training ground for sportsmen and women; and he would get to know it a lot better over the next two years. Attached to Lilleshall manor is what looks like a sports hall and accommodation block, much like what you'd find at a boarding school. There was a self-service restaurant, bar area, and bedrooms, which you either shared or had to yourself. Planted within the Lilleshall complex is a rehabilitation centre for the walking wounded of Britain's sporting elite. Men and women from different sports would come to recover while swapping war stories and comparing injuries. Foster found himself amid ten professional footballers, from the 30-year-old Second Division clogger who wanted three more years in the game to earn enough to look after his family, to the 70-grand-a-week star who relied on his talent.

As Foster regained fitness, he returned to Henley and jogged and cycled alongside the crew from which he was still exiled. Just before the FISA (governing body of world rowing) World Cup regatta at Munich in late May 1998, he and Grobler were following the four along the towpath, when Grobler turned to Foster.

'How do you think they are doing?'

'Not too well.'

Grobler nodded. 'We go to Munich with fingers crossed,' he said.

At Munich, the crew won their heat. Then Grobler swapped Grubor and Redgrave, putting Redgrave at 3 and Grubor at 2, breaking one of his own rules about quick-fix solutions, with the predictable result. In the final, they lay in third place after 500 metres, hauled themselves to second by halfway, but faded in the third 500 metres. They finished fourth, 6.71 seconds behind Romania, Germany and – shock – Poland. It was Redgrave's first taste of defeat in a championship race since 1990, and ended the four's eleven-strong run of victories. Foster watched Munich on television with a feeling of guilt and helplessness not unmingled with glee.

Afterwards, Pinsent said, 'The quality of crews we are up against this year is a different kettle of fish from 1997. We needed an excellent row to win and we had a bad one.'

To Foster this was merely evidence of how the crew were failing to realise how badly they were going, how much they needed him back, and how their shunning him was a sign of misplaced confidence.

The four returned to Leander in a mood of grim determination. They missed out the following round of the FISA World Cup at Hazewinkel in Belgium, where the Romanians were beaten by the Australians.

Grobler knew the four needed a fit Foster. It took all his wiles to reintroduce him. 'At the time,' said Grobler, 'James didn't want him back in the boat. But I started with Matthew. I did a little bit of shifting around. And finally . . .' A meeting took place in the Leander gym. Views were aired. Foster apologised.

'I'd put myself in a position where I was susceptible to an accident, and that was my fault,' he said.

'Yeah, we know, Tim,' said Redgrave breathing forgiveness. 'These things could happen to any of us, but it's not like he's done it deliberately.'

Six days after Munich, five weeks after the accident, Foster, healed, restored, scarred and forgiven, was back on board. Thereafter, his attitude shifted. He took a serious look at his non-rowing life.

'Previously I'd asked myself, "Will such-and-such activity harm my rowing?" Now, I began to ask myself, "Will this activity *help* my rowing?" It was a defining moment.'

Until then, Redgrave had tended to regard Foster as a lesser physical specimen. After Foster's restoration, he admitted he was wrong and that Foster was worth ten seconds over 2000 metres. If anything, Foster's reputation within the crew was enhanced. Not only did he have a personality the media could relate to, but the crew also realised they needed him.

The smell of spilt blood was enough to bring the Oarsome Foursome out of hibernation. They duly entered the Stewards' Challenge Cup at Henley Royal Regatta in July 1998. So did the Danish lightweight World Champions. The Australian challenge was eagerly awaited. The Oarsome Foursome were Olympic Champions, but hadn't raced abroad since 1996. Three of the Australian crew were Olympic Champions in 1992. The British held the Australians in greatest respect. Any crew containing James Tomkins, Mike McKay, Drew Ginn and Nick Green was potentially very slippery indeed. Tomkins was Australia's Redgrave; he would go on to win World Championship gold medals in every class of heavyweight sweep-oared boat. Mike McKay's character paralleled Redgrave's. The son of a builder (like Redgrave), McKay had something of Redgrave's determination that no one would beat him. This particular Australian four, who rowed under the colours of Mercantile Rowing Club from Melbourne, liked to play things their own way. Never a crew to peak early, they had been beaten at a selection trial in Australia by a rival four from Sydney, who went on to represent Australia in that year's World Championships. The British were more wary of this Melbourne-based four than the Sydney one. An epic clash was anticipated, billed as World Champions vs Olympic Champions. This time, the British four rowed as 'Leander Club'. Foster contemplated making a stand for Star Club in Bedford, of which he was a member, and petitioning to have the official entry as 'Leander Club & Star Rowing Club', but wisely decided that shutting up and fitting in was the better part of valour.

Leander drew the favoured Berkshire station, closest to the river bank (Henley is rowed against the stream, so that the crew on the bank-hugging Berkshire station has a marginal advantage over the crew on the Buckinghamshire station, which rows more or less along the centre of the river, where the stream is strongest). Sitting on the Start, McKay and Redgrave, in their respective 2 seats, shot each other glances, mutual acknowledgement of two great competitors.

Leander led by two feet at the top of Temple Island, some 30 strokes into the race, and by half a length at the Quarter-Mile. They passed the Barrier (about 500 metres into the race) one length up, in a time one second outside the record, despite a strong stream against them. The Australians made their move and began to inch back. By Fawley, they had pegged Leander's lead to three-quarters of a length. 'If they keep that speed up,' thought Foster, 'we're in trouble. I can't pull any harder and make the Finish.'

The Australians could indeed keep that speed up. By Remenham Club, they had clawed Leander back to half a length. The strains of 'Advance Australia Fair' began striking up. Still the Australians kept surging. At the Mile, Leander led by one third of a length. Passing the first of the enclosures, Mercantile had reeled in Leander to within a few feet, to gasps from the home crowd. The crews were so close, Mike McKay could hear the Leander four panting. A slight wash from a pleasure craft momentarily upset the Australian rhythm, just as Leander went for the line. A roar rose from the brilliant tangle of bright blazers as the crew drove the rate up to 42. Leander's one-length victory was marred by Pinsent luxuriously punching the air five strokes from the line, and punching it again once across the line. Mike Sweeney, the regatta chairman, later admonished him for this shocking breach of etiquette. 'I thought it was a juvenile action on Matt's part and totally unnecessary,' he said. No action was taken, and Pinsent admitted his gesture had been an instinctive reaction to the tension of the race.

Beating the Oarsome Foursome at Henley in 1998 was one of Cracknell's most satisfying races. 'He [Pinsent] is amazing in the way he raises his game,' he said. 'He brought us to another level ... At Henley, it feels more like rowing in a stadium. Normally, rowing a 2000 metre course, there's nobody until the last 250 metres, whereas at Henley there are people right from the Start. There's a special atmosphere and that was the first time I'd experienced it.'

'We were very pleased to win,' says Foster. 'We had become a four. Until then there had been a lot of talk of "Redgrave, Pinsent and two others". What had been established was that it was our four and not just Steve and Matthew with two guys holding it level.'

In the final of the Stewards' the following day, Leander met the Danish lightweight World Champions, unbeaten since 1995. Despite conceding 25 kilograms a man, the Danes were itching to take on the 'big men' of Leander. Leander took a slight lead off the Start. Blustery crosswinds upset their steering, but Leander led by three-quarters of a length at the Half-Mile. Approaching Fawley, Leander were warned by the umpire. At the Mile, Leander led by one length. Rating 42 along the enclosures, they won by three-quarters of a length but never felt threatened. 'People always say, "Those Danes gave you a great race," ' says Foster, 'but at no point did they go faster than us. The Australians were tougher. They raced to win, but lost by a larger distance because they'd gambled more.'

After further success at Lucerne International Regatta in mid-July, the crew went to the World Championships in Cologne in September 1998 as favourites. They began their opening heat in style. Norway and Egypt threw everything at them in the first 1000 metres, but the four pulled away, and cruised home rating 32 strokes per minute.

In the final, pouring rain and a howling tailwind turned Cologne into a winter wasteland with winning crews shivering on the rostrum. The race was a slog, but Great Britain held off pressure from Romania, Italy and France to win in a time of 5 minutes 48.06 seconds, just 0.17 seconds outside the world record.

It was a rugged, gut-busting performance by Britain in trying conditions. Redgrave later described it as an off day. 'We rowed very strongly over the first half of the race,' he said. 'But when it looked as if we were in control, it seemed to slip away. It was a pity we couldn't keep the race totally out of the hands of the others, but we didn't panic.'

'I remember the effort of Cologne after the grace and glide of Aiguebelette,' says Foster. 'We got up but couldn't get away. On form we could have won by a reasonable distance. We probably had one of our worst rows ever.'

'We had a poor row as a crew,' wrote Cracknell later, 'and personally I did not row the way I had visualised. The next time we raced I was determined we should demonstrate our best, dominate the race and not give other crews a sniff of us.'

Redgrave's win at Cologne made him the first oarsman to win eight world titles. To Cracknell, world titles were milestones in his life. To Redgrave they were like birthday cards. 'It's sad to say,' he said, 'but I don't quite get the same thrill from becoming World Champion that I used to. It's just something that has to be done. It is more of a marker, really. I've not consciously come here to win the world title. I've come here to keep on track for the Olympics. That is what I'm aiming for.'

In the three-week lull after Cologne, Redgrave, Pinsent and Foster couldn't get far enough away from a gym. Cracknell did a triathlon – 1500 metre swim, 40 kilometre bike ride and 10 kilometre run – for fun. 'I can see myself doing that when I've finished rowing,' he said. 'It was so foggy in the morning I got a bit lost and swam an extra lap more than I was supposed to.'

8

Cracknell and Pinsent: The Odd Couple

To Cracknell, whose hero was Nelson Mandela 'for never giving up in what he believed in and not being bitter afterwards', rowing was all about sacrifice. He was obsessed. Everything had to be on the edge physically. He could never take time off, could never resist the chance of bettering himself. If he could train that little bit harder, the boat would go that little bit faster. He'd pile on extra work and grow jittery if not training. Two weeks into a three-week break after one World Championships, he couldn't help going down to the gym to lift weights, which in his eyes didn't count. This was a chap whose teddy bear sleeps in a tracksuit. He describes himself as, 'Intense, frustrated, incredibly competitive, driven, quite emotional, hard to train with, but useful to have around, and at the same time fun to have around. I guess I'm a sports psychologist's dream patient.'

He didn't merely want to beat every other four in the world. He wanted to beat his crew-mates too. He felt threatened by Greg Searle, who, until Atlanta, outranked him in the squad pecking order.

He was a John Blunt figure, a mythical what-you-see-is-what-you-get Englishman who calls a spade a spade, has no pretensions, is brutally honest and never satisfied. He could be moody, less so within a group than with friends and family. He'd let his feelings be known and was always honest. His scull spent more time on trestles, being adjusted, than on the water.

Even rowing 16 kilometres on the ergometer machine as part of a third training session on a Thursday afternoon, he always made sure his ergo score edged Pinsent's. Such drive was terrific in a crew, but were you to put four Cracknells in a boat, it would implode. They would tear each other apart. A journalist asked him who had most influenced his career. 'Me,' he shot back. 'I'd definitely say I was self-motivated.'

When training in sculls, Foster, who knew a few tricks, would wind Cracknell up by asking open-ended questions such as, 'What do you think of last night's television?' or anything that required a long answer, just to test Cracknell's breath control. The first time Cracknell and Foster raced against each other in training was just before Henley Royal Regatta in 1997. Grobler asked them to scull four 2 kilometre pieces at UT1.

'No one beats me at UT1,' bragged Cracknell as he and Foster folded themselves into their sculling boats.

In their first piece, Foster took enormous pleasure in annoying Cracknell by taking the lead, adopting an air of studied casualness and careless grace while looking around and enjoying the scenery, which frustrated Cracknell even more. Cracknell complained that Foster was overrating him. John Pilgrim-Morris, a Leander coach on the bank, confirmed that Foster was in fact *under*rating Cracknell. Foster outperformed Cracknell in all four pieces. As they returned to the Leander landing stage, Redgrave cheerily greeted the scullers.

'Who won?' he called out.

'It wasn't a race,' smiled Foster, noting a thunderous scowl about to break on Cracknell's face. 'Just training.'

'That means you lost,' laughed Redgrave.

Foster kept quiet. He realised Cracknell had taken the episode far worse than expected. 'If you're training with James, he has to be one length up. It's what fuels him,' says Foster. 'I'd done to him what he'd do to others.'

Training camps brought out a loony fringe in Cracknell, especially Silvretta. He was always the first to leap fully nude into icy glacier-fed mountain torrents to ribald encouragement from fellow squad members, or undertake dares. A couple of years before the Atlanta Games, the squad stumbled on a live electric fence, and decided to wager who could grasp it in their hands for longest. Cracknell, who didn't have enough money to pay for his share of the satellite television card, won by clenching it between his teeth long enough to take several jolts ('I don't have any fillings, so there was a bit of logic there'). In 2000 Redgrave brought with him to Silvretta his diabetic's stabbing 'pencil' that he'd use to check his blood-sugar level. The squad bet Cracknell £10 he wouldn't stab the end of his penis. Cracknell happily carried out the dare, but refused to accept the cash because the stab hadn't been painful enough.

Arrogance and complacency were anathema to Cracknell. After each outing he'd ask Foster, 'How did it go?' Foster would make his comment, and a discussion would ensue. On training camps, where Foster and Cracknell traditionally room-shared, this discussion might drag on until well after lights-out. A recurrent theme was, 'Matthew not pulling his weight.'

Pinsent was competitive too, but in a different way. His hero was another boat-mover and leader of men: Ernest Shackleton, for 'courage in the face of almost overwhelming adversity'.

'Matthew is perhaps the most difficult to summarise,' says Foster, who had known Pinsent the longest of all the crew – ever since 1987 when they had won gold at the World Junior

Championships in a pair. 'He kept himself to himself, and would never talk about personal matters or what he did away from rowing, unlike the rest of us. A tour around James Cracknell was an open-top-bus ride; a journey around Matthew Pinsent was a voyage into the unknown. Pinsent is an introverted extrovert.'

He was never quite as hooked on rowing as the others, or didn't appear to be. With Matthew, the gap between where he thought he was and where he wanted to be was much smaller than was the case with his crew-mates. As a result, he exuded self-confidence. He would far rather have been known as overconfident than not. Foster had known him before he had acquired this confidence, but the years of gold-medal-winning rowing glory during the 1990s had given that confidence a permanent berth in Pinsent's psyche. Cracknell described him as, 'More of an extrovert [than Redgrave] and extremely confident, both in life and in his own athletic ability. He does not suffer fools or time-wasters very easily, which sometimes may give people the wrong impression. He is possibly not as competitive in training as Steve, but he has the best British rowing record.'

A characteristic of many confident people is that they have blind spots, and some of Pinsent's wrapped round through 360 degrees. 'If we were all sitting in a room, while someone else was watching television,' says Foster, 'Matthew would unthinkingly get up and switch it off without realising someone else was watching it.' The blind spots extended to the tactical minutiae of rowing, which luckily for Pinsent was Redgrave's speciality.

'Matthew doesn't allow the phrase "self-doubt" to exist in his life and doesn't think he needs it,' says Rachel Quarrell. 'The difference between him and Steve is that Steve has a lot of self-doubt. It's what makes Steve more aware. Steve will always be thinking about everything, the wind, the stream,

"Can I change when I train?", "Would it help to get someone else to look at the boat?" ' Pinsent and Redgrave's attitudes to racing differed markedly. To Redgrave losing, or even coming second, could be re-patterned as a learning curve; to Pinsent failure was the pits. He didn't believe in coming second. If you couldn't be the best at something, it wasn't worth doing at all. It was win or bust.

'He's basically a nice bloke who doesn't always give a good first impression,' says Foster. 'I wouldn't describe him as a real team player. At times, he'll do a lot for a friend, like lend his house or car. At other times, he won't, or won't be bothered.'

Pinsent's rowing style was unorthodox. He leant into his rigger and finished each stroke with a great wrench of his outside shoulder. Any technical coach, unaware of his for-midable record, would be tempted to take his style to pieces and rebuild it. But clearly it worked.

He was also on the lazy side of economical in his approach. (He admitted to the *Evening Standard* he could 'idle for England ... I could loaf about all day without worrying about doing anything.' At training camps, his ability to fall asleep given a flat surface and twenty minutes earned him the nick-name 'Rip van Pinsent'.) While others put themselves on the line day after day to achieve results, Pinsent put himself on the line when it counted, once every four years. He trained, but only just. He rarely *engaged* in the programme. Some mornings, as the four plodded along admiring the view, the crew felt Pinsent was going through the motions. Cracknell, who made the calls during training outings, would shout, 'Push with the legs.' A minute or two later, after receiving no obvious response, he'd repeat, 'Push with the legs!!' Pinsent would then start to ignore Cracknell.

During one outing in the four, the crew attached a speed-ometer to the hull of the boat. This tiny impeller measures the boat's speed through the water. At UT2, Grobler wanted the crew to move the boat at a rate of between 1 minute 51 seconds and 1 minute 59 seconds per 500 metres on a 20 kilometre outing. Pinsent argued that it wasn't possible to pull the boat that fast over that distance. This puzzled Foster and Cracknell. That's what they'd been doing in their pair all season. Grobler pointed out to Pinsent that that was the whole point of training. This was typical of Pinsent's approach to training. On days when he was switched on, 1 minute 51 seconds per 500 metres was easy; on days when he wasn't, the boat would feel heavy and lifeless. The crew even invented a new level of training especially for Pinsent: UT3.

Pinsent disliked sculling. He wasn't the best at it so he thought it a waste of time. One day, training at Henley, Grobler told Pinsent to scull two 1000 metre pieces. Matthew stepped into his boat, pushed off, sculled the first 1000 metres, turned around, sculled the second 1000 metres and came home. Redgrave could never have done that; Redgrave would have needed to paddle the full length of the river at Henley just to get properly warmed up and sculling at full-reach.

Pinsent's performances in the gym were another matter. Awesomely powerful and endowed with freakish aerobic capacity, he could outlift the squad and post phenomenal long-distance ergometer scores. After an outing in 1997 the crew was summoned to take part in an ergometer trial. While Redgrave, Cracknell and Foster took time out to psych themselves up, Pinsent leapt straight on to the rowing machine, did his trial, jumped off it and had returned home before the rest of the crew had even begun their tests.

'Matthew is too good for his own good,' says Foster. 'Were he less good, he might try harder. You need a cattle prod to get him going. On the ergometer, he could pull as hard as my maximum without breaking into a sweat. If I am lifting my maximum weight, you couldn't add another gram. But if

Jürgen loaded another 20 kilograms on to Matthew's maximum, he'd protest – "Oh Jürgen, I can't lift that" – then lift it easily.' An inspired Pinsent, however, was a 'very different beast to the unthinking just-got-out-of-bed Pinsent', says Foster. 'It was fantastic to have him on your side when it counted.'

Pinsent's approach was antipodes apart from Cracknell's. Sometimes Cracknell thought Pinsent was coasting, and tried to rub it in. He would almost sacrifice himself to prove that Matthew was slacking. Over meetings in the Leander Porta-kabin, Cracknell would wind Pinsent up. Sometimes this ploy worked positively, at others it would annoy. Redgrave would step in and tell this ingénue spaniel to calm down.

In the build-up to the 1998 World Championships in Cologne, Cracknell kept complaining about the boat. Redgrave snapped. 'If you haven't got anything positive to say, don't say it! Don't always look for things that aren't there!'

Cracknell took it well, and Pinsent and Redgrave appre-ciated and fed off James's motivation – 'Things Matthew and I might have taken for granted, he made sure we didn't miss out on,' said Redgrave – but not necessarily at the same time.

The sources of Pinsent's seemingly effortless power weren't hard to find, and the place to find them was at the British Olympic Medical Centre at Northwick Park Hospital in north-west London. Three times each year, between November and Easter, the crew would travel there and submit to a lactate test. This was a test of the intensity at which the crew was working. When you row on an ergometer machine – or take any form of strenuous exercise – the body produces lactic acid, which gets into the bloodstream and makes your muscles hurt. You can measure the intensity at which the body is working by measuring the amount of lactic acid in the blood. Hence the lactate test, one of the most hellish among Grobler's repertoire of tortures.

To reach the Medical Centre, you walked through the main part of Northwick Park Hospital in Harrow, round a back corner and along a passage, while looking out for five Olympic rings on the wall. Inside the centre were two large laboratories, five consulting rooms, and a main reception area. In one laboratory stood two rowing ergometer machines, a cycling ergometer, two treadmills, a canoe ergometer, several computers and a worrying-looking contraption called the 'respiratory analyser'. This took the form of a computer with bell jars attached that measured the amount of oxygen you breathed in and the amount of carbon dioxide you breathed out.

It was an uncomfortable machine. You bit on a snorkel-like mouthpiece, which had two pipes leading off to these bell jars. You strapped yourself on to an ergometer machine, while a white smock wired you up to an electrocardiogram and pegged your nostrils to prevent you breathing through your nose. You then rowed for four minutes. During a thirty-second breather, a white smock would take a blood sample from your ear. Then you'd row another four minutes at greater intensity, then rest another thirty seconds while they took another sample, and so on, until you'd rowed six four-minute pieces, each one at a higher tempo than the one before, until your face was contorted in a rictus of agony – or would have been were it not for this infernal snorkel thing stuck in your mouth. The tubes, being quite narrow, constricted the flow of air, making breathing hard work and inducing a disquieting sense of asphyxiation, which is the last thing you want when rowing flat out on an ergometer. On top of the pain and the nose-pegging and the sense of suffocation was the dribbling. You couldn't stop yourself slavering down the tubes. It was really most unpleasant.

'The four of us would take the test in turn,' says Foster. 'I would arrive just as James was finishing his final four minutes.

Throughout the last minute, his face was white and his lips turned blue as the oxygen in his body rushed to his muscles. He would then collapse, still wired up to the electrocardiogram sensors. I never saw Matthew push himself that far.'

The respiratory analyser wasn't as much a test of character as the ergometer machine, and it certainly had nothing to do with oarsmanship. For gifted underweights like Foster, it was a humiliating exercise. When Foster first undertook the lactate test, his figures were so poor that Grobler took him aside and said, 'How can anyone with scores like yours call himself an international oarsman?'

Among Grobler's minimum criteria for an Olympic oarsman was an ability to generate no less than 350 watts of power at the 'four millimole' level of lactic acid in the blood. In twelve lactate tests, Foster achieved this only once. He would fare appallingly badly, yet could still move a boat quicker than almost anyone in the squad, thanks largely to his technique but also to his heart rate, which could rise from reptilian lows to a dizzying 195 and stay there for prolonged periods. Foster was ready to diss the lactate test, but Grobler persuaded him that if his scores improved, he'd be a better boat-mover.

Northwick Park also measured the crew's lung capacity. Foster's and Cracknell's were about 6 litres. Redgrave measured about 6.5 litres. Back in 1996, Bruce Davies, white-smock-in-chief, looked up from his lung capacity charts and confirmed that Redgrave was indeed one of the fittest athletes he'd ever come across. 'But not as fit as that one,' he added, pointing to Pinsent pulling an ergometer to pieces in the middle of the lab. Pinsent's lungs were a breathtaking and no doubt environmentally destabilising 8.5 litres, the largest ever recorded at the Medical Centre. Physically, he was a monster. He proved so strong that his power output went right off the dial. They actually had to recalibrate the machine, because his body only got going when most others were ready to throw in the towel. Grobler said Pinsent should run in the Derby not row in the Olympics.

Another Northwick Park ordeal was the calliper test to measure fat deposits. Measurements were taken by pinching the biceps, triceps, the back of the shoulder blade and the 'love handles'. Redgrave registered low measurements on the first three, but his love handles let him down. Pinsent measured high scores all round, especially on triceps, the back part of the upper arm. As the squad put it, he had 'bingo arms'.

9

Spine Chiller

October 1998

In the last week of October the four were doing some pieces of flat-out work at Henley in preparation for the Fours Head of the River in London. Halfway through one piece, Foster's back went *ping!* and seized up. He could hardly move. Redgrave and Cracknell rowed the boat back to Leander with Foster grimacing in agony. At the Leander landing stage, Foster was unable to stand up straight.

He'd felt rumblings in his back ever since training had resumed on 1 October 1998. Each morning the physiotherapist would stretch him out on the floor of the Leander gym. Not that he had a problem, you understand: it was merely part of his warm-up routine; but this was the latest instalment in an ongoing back drama that had more twists and turns than the Thames.

The lumbar spine is the Achilles heel of oarsmen. During the rowing stroke, the spine links the leg-drive with the draw of the arms and shoulders. At the same time it flexes and twists in an 'unnatural' movement which, repeated millions of times, the body can't stand. Had God intended human beings to row, he'd have given them one arm longer than the other, and vertebrae made of titanium.

Foster's spine was a recurrent nightmare. Just before Lucerne International Regatta in July '92 – an important trial regatta before the Barcelona Olympics – it had gone *ping!* as he sat in a bus en route to training. 'I couldn't move. This was one week before a selection regatta. On Tuesday, after physiotherapy, I flew to Lucerne. I could walk, but not bend over. By Wednesday, my back was mobile. By Thursday, I was rowing. By Friday, I was racing. The pressure was on. I'd feel fine one minute, then jagged pains would shoot from toes to shoulders the next.'

Later that year, after Barcelona, a scan had shown two bulging discs in the lower lumbar spine. Surgeons had removed one of them in October '93. Foster took six months to recover and resumed training. Being short of one disc, the muscles in his lumbar region tended to seize up to protect his spine, causing his hamstrings to tighten. To ensure sufficient flexibility in his back, merely to allow the normal range of movements, required continual stretching.

In this latest episode his specialist found a bulge in one disc and an annular tear in another, which had prolapsed and was causing Foster to walk crookedly. Foster reckoned he knew what had brought it on. The year before, playing cricket at altitude training camp in Austria, he had launched into a 'spectacular diving catch'. As he put his foot down, the ground had proved further away than he'd thought, and he'd jarred his back on landing.

Foster rushed to Lilleshall Rehabilitation Centre. The doctors administered an epidural. By early December he felt fine. He'd recovered. The night before he was due to resume training, the telephone rang at his Oxford house. He took the call sitting on the staircase. When he'd finished speaking and put down the receiver, he found he couldn't stand up. His back had gone – again. He rang Ann Redgrave. She was out, so he left a message. When she picked up the message, she assumed Foster was ringing to say he felt fine. Instead, when she returned his call, she heard: 'Something has gone wrong. I can't move.'

Tuesday, 15 December 1998

Foster's specialist was Matt Stallard – in his sixties, an ex-oarsman, tall (6 feet 6 inches), very matter-of-fact, so much so that he would often forget to tell you the crucial details of your condition. The first fifteen minutes of a twenty-minute consultation were always spent talking rowing, until finally . . . 'So how's the back?'

He examined Foster at Harpenden Hospital in Hertfordshire. 'You can either bugger about,' he concluded, 'which we have already tried. Or you can bugger off. Or we can take the disc out. What are you doing on Friday?'

'Bugger about' meant injections and intensive physio-therapy, which weren't working. 'Bugger off' meant give up rowing, and hope that the problem would disappear. Taking the disc out meant another operation. He never said, 'Don't row,' or, 'Yes, you can row,' or, 'You're fine.' His advice was: 'Read the signs. Only you can tell.'

Foster reckoned that after his previous back operation he'd had an 80 per cent chance of making a recovery. With a second similar operation and the same odds, he therefore had a 64 per cent chance of full recovery; but if it worked it was better than the 'bugger about' option.

'To be fair,' prompted Stallard, 'you can't even do normal things at the moment. There are two stages of being: one is being a normal person; the other is being an Olympic athlete. If you could achieve normal-person movement in your back, the decision would be whether you wanted to go through all this and become an Olympic athlete, but you can't even achieve normality.'

That made Foster's decision easier. The disc would have to go. It was holding him back. Dr Ann Redgrave, who as team doctor was effectively Foster's too, was outwardly positive but inwardly concerned.

Foster left Harpenden Hospital with a feeling of black emptiness. He sat in his Lombard-sponsored car in the car park while he saw his world crumbling around him. The dream still burned in him, but his body had let him down.

After fifteen minutes' staring in near cataleptic gloom out of his windscreen, Foster made a conscious effort to perk himself up. He fired the engine, put his car into gear and drove off. He hadn't travelled more than 200 metres when he came to a zebra crossing. And old woman was waiting to cross. He stopped. As the old lady crossed at 0 mph, Foster noticed she seemed so pleased that he'd stopped. She waved thanks. That made him feel sorry at having felt so selfish about himself. *What's a word beginning with 'self' and ending with 'pitying'?* he wondered.

He realised that things weren't as bad as he was making them out to be. That he was aspiring to do the extraordinary meant that he shouldn't be filled with self-pity if he could only achieve the ordinary. He knew the operation would eventually cure the pain. The question was: would he row again, with a 64 per cent chance?

Friday, 18 December

Foster awoke from the anaesthetic at Harpenden Hospital, minus a second piece of his spine. His father drove him to the family seat in Bedford, where he lay supine on his parents' sofa for two months, staring at the ceiling as if for forensic evidence that he had once been an international oarsman and held his own in a boat where he had sat between two of the greatest legends in the history of his sport. Yet here he was, in a state of near-paralysis, with the Olympics twenty-one months away.

Having had a similar operation in 1993, he knew what to expect: the uncertainty of not knowing which movements he could get away with, and which movements would trigger screaming pain, the difficulty of simple tasks like standing up and rolling over in bed, the slow recovery and exercise regime.

He could hardly bear to roll over. The pain of swinging his legs round and heaving his body over was so great that he lay in the same position for hours, whereupon his body would seize up. He had to plan in advance when to roll over, calling his mother in to help. Heather Foster would watch helplessly as Foster shut his eyes and quivered in yellow pain.

An international athlete, accustomed to six hours' training each day and the outdoor life, Foster felt like a caged animal committed to being indoors for twenty-four hours a day. Through his parents' sitting-room window he saw people strolling merrily past along the pavement and thought how remote and alien the mere act of walking seemed. As for contemplating the movements of rowing, the very thought of them inspired pain. The worst times were when the painkillers were either wearing off or hadn't yet cut in, when he simply had to lie and suffer.

Foster spent Christmas Day flat on his back. The dinner table was moved into the sitting room. Foster's mother, father (Brian) and elder brother (Jason) took their places while Foster himself lay down and tried to digest his turkey and stuffing in a horizontal position. When he was able to stand on his feet, he walked inch by inch like a 100-year-old man. Mere pigeon steps were, for him, great leaps forward; but he kept having to stop while lightning bolts zigzagged down his spine and he would whiten and start quivering. Simply moving from the bedroom to the sitting room required considerable planning.

Foster had always thought he was good at going through

the pain barrier, in rowing at least; but this was screaming pain of a different dimension. Rowing had taught him about self-inflicted extremes of discomfort aimed at achieving fantastic goals, but when the pain came as a result of pushing himself through mere normality, it was confusing.

He knew the palsying agony would eventually cease, but not until several unpleasant weeks had elapsed. Yet he still found himself hungering after Olympic gold. He still saw himself mounting shallow steps to the rostrum and watching the Union flag rise. He knew the feeling of being there and hearing 'God Save the Queen' would be so much greater and so much more exhilarating because of what he'd been through in order to achieve it. But in order to grasp that gold medal, he'd have to breach a wall of fire.

'It made it so much harder to achieve, but made me want it so much more,' he said. 'It wasn't just an Olympic gold medal but a battle against the odds, a nigh-on impossibility to do it at that point. At the same time, the very thought of rowing made me feel sick. If you imagine having your hand crushed in a mangle, you'd cringe at the thought. For me, rowing had the same effect. Just watching people do it hurt.'

He kept in touch with the crew by telephone. Their tales of three training sessions a day seemed very remote from Foster's tentative first steps and long hours spent staring at daytime television. He was so out of touch with the 7.30 a.m. starts that he scarcely believed Redgrave when he rang having completed the day's training, while he, Foster, was still at breakfast. He surrendered to a very different pace of invalid life, trading 20 kilometre outings and reckonings with the ergo for the daily challenge of pulling on socks while hobbling from bedroom to sitting room.

Foster's New Year was less about exercising than about performing simple manoeuvres and achieving pain-free movement. Early progress was measured in pathetically small increments, such as rolling over, touching his knees, and pulling on trousers. Flexibility was never his forte, but he could at least see his feet – that's if he could get the tube of blubber he was carrying out of the way.

The first time he stepped outside the house, three weeks after his operation, was a triumphant moment. On 21 January he was well enough to pay his Bedford physiotherapist James Burrell a visit. He tried to convince Burrell that he felt fine.

'OK,' said Burrell, 'take your shoes off and let's have a look at you.'

'Ah.' There was no way Foster could do that. He was bluffing, way out of his depth. Burrell ended up removing his shoes for him.

This time, the crew were more understanding. They even sent him a card.

When sufficient mobility was restored, Foster bought an aquajog – a harness that held him vertically in water, allowing him to 'run' without jarring his spine. He went to his local swimming pool, donned the aquajog and jumped in. 'Everyone gave me very strange looks,' he says. 'I "jogged" so slowly that grannies keeping their hair dry would overtake me.'

Redgrave, Pinsent and Cracknell seemed a million miles away. In fact, they were 10,500 miles away on training camp in Australia, visiting the Olympic Village, stadium and Penrith. One glimpse of the 2000 metre lake stretching out into seeming infinity sent a shiver up Cracknell's spine. 'As we turned into Sydney regatta park,' he wrote, 'my adrenaline levels soared. This is where it will take place. It seemed strange seeing it so quiet, but I could visualise it packed with grandstands on both sides and spectators right up to the start, and us paddling out to race . . . the three of us met up in the grandstand to look out over the course. Not a lot was said, we all knew what was going to happen in 21 months' time and how it would affect our lives.'

The training camp took place at Hinze Dam, just inland from the Gold Coast, a scenic and relatively deserted spot chosen for its climate, proximity to Sydney and relaxed environment, to which the British crews had exclusive access, the British Olympic Association having swung a deal with Gold Coast City Council, in which they agreed to spend £500,000 helping upgrade the facilities, including a running track, hockey stadium and 50 metre pool. The dam itself was a protected expanse suitable for short and long-distance rowing events. In the surrounding flat countryside, Grobler even managed to find a hill suitable for cycling sorties. The Australian rowing team had wanted to train at Hinze too, but the Gold Coast authorities banned its use by the Australians, even on a temporary basis. It was a blissful spot.

The boys rubbed it in by sending Foster a postcard of a topless Australian beauty, and rang him helpfully to point out that the temperature in Celsius in Australia was numerically the same as in Fahrenheit in England.

January 1999

Foster's hopes of rejoining the squad altitude training camp in the Sierra Nevada, in the Spanish mountains, proved wildly optimistic. He had mountains of a different sort to climb. Yet another sojourn at Lilleshall beckoned.

Physiotherapists nursed him through the first steps back into training, beginning with cycling. 'After two hours on my bike, straining against the wind, my legs and face are frozen, my hands and feet dropped off an hour ago,' he wrote in his diary. 'I am soaked to the skin from incessant rain. But I am happy. The one thing that I can't feel during this, my first training session for four months, is my back.'

Once more, he found himself tossed among a hobbling band of happy-go-lucky footballers, rugby players and cricketers, a few of whom even recognised him, which came as a boost. He patiently, and using words of not more than two syllables, explained how rowing works. 'They didn't realise that formations are as important in rowing as in football,' he says. 'I compared Matthew with Alan Shearer – very reliable and leads the line. Behind him is myself, a kind of creative midfielder, a David Beckham, skilful despite occasional lapses into career-threatening stupidity. Then there's Steve, the Tony Adams figure, the motivator who leads the back and gets stuck in, and James, the bowman, who is David Seaman, the last line of defence.'

He explained how crews are far more delicate mechanisms than football teams. Moulding together styles and characters, while forging a rhythm, takes time. Success is measured not only in defeat or victory at races, but also in less quantifiable factors such as fluency and the 'feel' of a boat.

They unanimously greeted Foster's training with a mix of horrified fascination and gobsmacked disbelief. How they laughed when he returned, purple-faced and frozen-fingered, from three-hour cycling marathons in blizzard conditions. They thought Foster was mad. They couldn't work out why he was so dedicated for no financial reward.

'If the gaffer's not looking, I'd jack it in,' they'd say.

'I won't get another chance of Olympic gold,' replied Foster.

Still, it made you think. Those wise monkeys sitting in judgement had a point. Who in their right mind would spend twenty of the best years of their life striving for a fifth Olympic gold medal?

Britain is far better at rowing than at football, cricket and rugby, thought Foster. *Perhaps there's a masochistic low-self-esteem public-school-ethos streak lurking in the recesses of our national psyche.*

Foster had visited many beautiful places in his career, by no means all of them airport terminals and concrete rowing lakes, but nowhere he'd rather live than in England. Sometimes you had to travel abroad to appreciate your country; but just because you put your body on the line for your country, it doesn't follow that your country appreciates you. For the most part, the only response Foster had received for his efforts with an oar was yawning indifference. After Atlanta, there was a media-inspired feeling that Britain's athletes had failed their country; but they had done their best on meagre resources. Foster sometimes envied the popular support of athletes in, say, Australia.

'When people ask me what I do, I either reply, "Not a lot," or, "Full-time athlete," which to most people suggests track and field. If I say "rower", I often have to explain myself. The usual response is a strange look, then, "Is that all?" or, "Nice hobby." As with many minor sports, the nation only supports rowing during the Olympics or the Boat Race, but forgets about it immediately afterwards. After the Atlanta Olympics in 1996, Michelle de Bruin, the discredited Irish swimmer, was greeted by 5000 fans at Dublin airport; when Steve arrived home with Britain's only gold medal, six people turned up, five of them family. Were I as good at football as at rowing, I'd be a household name.

'I alternate between two views of rowing. On the one hand, it is nothing special in terms of what I'm educated for, and I certainly don't want to be known as just a rower. On the other hand, it is something I am very good at, good enough to be a World and perhaps Olympic Champion. I'm not Mr Average Rower. I'm better than average. That's what makes it worthwhile. I want to be the best at what I do, not the most famous. I would have loved to be a footballer, but I'm not good enough. I was in the school team at most sports, but never the star, except at rowing.

'Why do I not want to be known as a rower when I devote my life to it? Were I described as "a rower", I'd feel affronted.

I know a lot of World Champions, and in some way you want to be better than them. Strangely, I don't mind being known as a failed rock musician or a frustrated professional football player. But I'd hate to be known as a failed potential Olympic gold-medallist oarsman. Maybe I look down on lesser oarsmen more than on average footballers. In a bizarre way it would be worse to have tried and failed at rowing than to have tried and failed at the guitar, because I never gave the guitar a chance. Steve's the same. He'd like to be more than just a rower. He wants to be the greatest-ever Olympian. He's not necessarily relating to Joe Public. He's relating to Matthew. It's the same for all of us. Maybe part of us despises the fact that we've picked the wrong sport to be great at.

'I could never envisage rowing for any other reason than that I love it. You don't get famous or rich, or kudos. I do it because I enjoy it. If I didn't enjoy it, I wouldn't do it so well. I want desperately to win an Olympic gold medal. I know it's a cliché but you don't know how often I have dreamt of it. A lot of people say, "I dream of winning a gold medal." I've got close. I know what it entails. It *is* possible. It is just a question of getting it together.'

Is it surprising people think oarsmen are slightly mad?

Not that Foster's musical career was an entirely closed book, not yet. His pop group, Sexual Panther, had indeed once existed, when he was a student at London University. The University Boathouse in Chiswick, west London, was the perfect place to practise, having no immediate neighbours. Later on, at Oxford University, one of his fellow rowing squad members played the guitar. 'To call it music would be stretching even the loosest definition of music,' he says. 'We could never find anyone who could sing. I tried but couldn't, although I looked the part.'

Maybe it was time to dust off the musical career once more? For his thirtieth birthday, Foster was given a singing lesson.

It was one of the most embarrassing experiences to which he'd admit. 'This very nice lady who lived outside Oxford and who "refined" professional singers, was confronted by me,' he says. 'When I told her that I didn't necessarily aspire to being an opera singer, she thought I was being modest. Two bars of "Yesterday" saw to that. "A brave choice of song," she said, politely. I was old enough to have known better; I cannot say I was dragged there kicking and screaming by my parents.'

Late February 1999

Although keen to have Foster back, Grobler told him he was a human being first and an oarsman second. To take Foster's place, Grobler chose Ed Coode, son of a Cornish solicitor, who read marine biology at Newcastle University and who flew kites as a hobby. Charming, polite, well-scrubbed, placid, a credit to Eton College, he turned into a foaming zealot whenever the struggle for Cornish independence was raised. His sculling blades and the stern of his sculling boat were emblazoned with St Piran's flag after the patron saint of tin miners. Two years earlier, Coode had found himself in one of the lowliest of eights competitions at Newcastle University. A lucky break with a crew from the University of London had propelled him to a silver medal in the World Under-23 Championships, rowing in a coxed four. He had rowed for Oxford in the Boat Race of 1998. Now he had a sniff of Olympic gold. Ironically, he'd spent the previous year trying to emulate Foster's technique, having pored over footage of Foster in action, thinking, 'That's it! That's how I want to row!' He proved a better fit than Luka Grubor.

Foster could talk bravely of spending the winter improving fitness in time for the traditional ARA selection regatta in April, but he knew his rowing career hung by a thread marginally thinner than what remained of his spine. He was increasingly beginning to resemble the 'fifth Beatle' of the original Fab Four, the one no one can remember.

The squad attended at the two-day FISA Team Cup regatta at Seville, held over 500 metres and 1000 metres. Seville was a terrific place to row: thirteen uninterrupted kilometres of calm water and a clement winter climate. No British venue could compare.

The four, with Coode up, won on both days, beating the Danish lightweight four twice. It seemed like business as usual (*Tim who . . .?*). For Cracknell, the greatest difference between rowing with Coode as opposed to Foster was the change of room-mate. Foster's Spandau Ballet CD collection, chromatically uncomplementary wardrobe and ironic shoe fetishism were replaced by Ed Coode's latest must-read books and more conventional attire. 'I've convinced him that my CDs deserve priority on the stereo and that I beat him on Playstation or he can't use it,' wrote Cracknell. 'He gets his own back by falling asleep instantly and snoring.'

Wednesday, 17 March 1999

Ten days after the squad returned from Spain, Foster addressed a rowing boat for the first time in nearly four months. He had hoped no one would notice him hiding behind his scull as he tiptoed with it out of the Leander boathouse, but the squad turned out in force.

'Oh,' said Cracknell, in his best David Attenborough voice. 'We don't see a Foster down here much these days.'

In fact, Foster wanted to be, if not welcomed back, then at least seen to be training again. Coaches and fellow athletes so easily slip into an 'out of sight, out of shape' mindset when an athlete is absent. Watching Coode, the patient usurper, had spurred Foster. It reminded him of what he missed: Pinsent and his bacon sandwiches, the games of 'Guess the blood sugar level', the banter of crew-mates, Cracknell and his so-called balanced diet and amino acids – Cracknell would oscillate from one dietary fad to the next depending on which daytime television programme he'd been watching. One week he might eat the yolks of eggs only; the next week, he might eat the whites only. That Cracknell could follow two entirely contradictory diets from one week to the next without seeing the hypocrisy of it or the bigger picture would wind Redgrave up no end.

As he had done after his accident with the window pane the year before, Foster pushed the thin grey negotiable area between his rowing life and his private life further in favour of rowing. He curfewed his evenings, turned down invitations, renounced the world and tucked himself up in bed well *before* closing time. He dedicated himself absolutely and inseducibly. He became, in short, exactly the type of rower he'd always dreaded becoming. 'Previously, I wanted to be a rower first and foremost, but also to be known as something else too,' he says. 'From then on, I wanted to be solely a rower.'

He would arrive at Leander half an hour earlier than the squad to stretch and do mobility exercises, transverse abdominals and trunk rotation. (Grobler, who prided himself on turning up before everyone else, seized this as a challenge, and would arrive even earlier.) Foster was fired by a sense of abandonment by his former crew-mates. A card was fine, but where were the flowers and grapes? 'Had they gone through what I'd been through,' he fumed, 'I'd have shown more care.'

April 1999

Foster was ready to return to the fray, but when he lobbied the coaches and management team, they laughed and told him to get back into his sculling boat. Foster sat out the ARA selection regatta at Holmepierrepoint, in which the squad paired off and raced over 2000 metres.

Other absentees at this selection regatta were Greg Searle and Matthew Pinsent. This rather spoilt the fun. Coode and Cracknell were looking forward to racing Pinsent and Redgrave in the pair. A cracking race seemed in prospect, if their respective training times were any guide. There was an even greater prize at stake. The winners of the ARA pairs trials were traditionally allocated the only bedroom at Silvretta that contained two single beds, as opposed to one double. It also had the biggest and best Alpine views.

Ever-present, however, was Holmepierrepoint's notorious microclimate, which put on a thrilling display of sleet, snow, rain, sunshine and blustery winds all within a few minutes of each other. As the wind whipped up, it made the course unfair for multi-lane racing, so the opening heat was replaced by a time trial. Coode and Cracknell won. They also won the semi-final the following morning, and the final. That was bad news for Foster.

May 1999

The first international regatta of the summer was at Hazewinkel in Belgium. Those same coaches who had scorned Foster's attempted comeback now told him they'd entered him in the single scull. It was Foster's turn to laugh.

'You're joking.' The single scull was the toughest discipline in rowing. Not one for bad backs.

'Oh, you know me, Tim,' chortled Grobler. 'I don't joke.'

He had two weeks to prepare. He hastily scheduled his comeback in elite sculls at the two-day Metropolitan Regatta on Royal Albert Dock, on 22 May 1999, which was cancelled owing to strong winds.

Coode, meanwhile, could hardly believe his luck. Having been drafted on board in the winter of 1998, he was surprised to find himself still there the following summer; but, as Pinsent

The crew loosened up before outings in their own ways: here in Seville, Steve Redgrave and Tim Foster stretch hamstrings; James Cracknell carries the blades to the water; Matthew Pinsent keeps watch.

At the crew's debut in April 1997 at Henley, Steve Redgrave rowed at bow and James Cracknell at two; they eventually swapped positions in the final seating order.

Steve Redgrave shakes with Stewart Legg of Lombard Finance after announcing his comeback for the Sydney Olympics in 2000. Delightedly looking on are (*from left*) David Tanner, International Manager of the Amateur Rowing Association, Jürgen Grobler, Chief Coach, Matthew Pinsent and Dr Ann Redgrave.

Steve Redgrave juggles the Stewards' Challenge Cup at prize-giving at Henley Royal Regatta in 1997 watched by (*from left*) HRH the Duke of Edinburgh, Mike Sweeney (Chairman of HRR, obscured by post), James Cracknell, Tim Foster and Matthew Pinsent.

⋏ Matthew Pinsent's air-punch during the final of the Stewards' Challenge Cup at Henley Royal Regatta in 1998 earned him a reprimand. The four beat the reigning Olympic champions, the Oarsome Foursome from Australia, in their first race since Tim Foster's recovery from a hand injury.

Jürgen Grobler in the ➤ Leander Club boat bay during Henley Royal Regatta wearing his pink Leander Club tie and socks.

In May 1999, ➤ a trim Tim Foster relaunches his career after recovering from back surgery.

⋎ In training at Seville, Matthew Pinsent (*far right*), who never lacked basic nutrition, tucks into a cake, while James Cracknell (*far left*) and Steve Redgrave take on fluid.

In their last race on British waters, the crew powers off the Start in the final of the Stewards' Challenge Cup at Henley Royal Regatta in 2000. They beat the Australian coxless four by three-quarters of a length.

(*left to right*) Steve, Matthew and Tim show their golfing skills. The ball is actually stuck to the club with Blu Tack.

What a difference four years makes: (*top*) Tim Foster applauds the gold-medal winning Australian coxless four – the Oarsome Foursome – at the Atlanta Olympics in 1996, while disappointed crewmates Greg Searle, Jonny Searle and Rupert Obholzer look thunderously on; (*above*) Steve Redgrave, Tim Foster, James Cracknell and Matthew Pinsent celebrate winning gold in the same race at Sydney in 2000. Redgrave and Pinsent always took care never to stand next to each other in crew shots in case picture editors cropped out 'the other two'.

◁ Tim Foster celebrates gold with his father Brian, who, with his mother Heather, are his most loyal fans.

▽ In December 2000, Steve Redgrave finally, after years of near misses, lands the one trophy that had eluded him for years: the BBC Sports Personality of the Year. Ironically, in 2003, he topped a poll to pick the ultimate BBC's Sports Personality of the Year winner, in celebration of the award's 50th birthday.

Top: Exhaustion clearly beginning to show in the crew's technique and body angles during the last few strokes of the final of the coxless fours at Sydney. The Italian silver medallists are in the foreground; the bow of the Australian boat in between.

Above: The crew made its final journey in November 2000 when they paddled their coxless four 500 metres upstream from the Leander Club to its final resting place at the River & Rowing Museum at Henley, where they were greeted by Adrian Morris (*far left*), owner of Aylings who built the boat, and Paul Mainds, chief executive of the River & Rowing Museum (*far right*).

said of Coode, 'You wouldn't know there was a substitute on board.' (*Ah*, was Foster's response, *if Pinsent finds it just as comfortable with Coode, that's because Coode has the same faults as Pinsent*.) Coode rowed in the four throughout that season, starting with the Hazewinkel regatta. Drawing on the previous season's faltering experience with Luka Grubor, when the crew, either through complacency or whatever, had lost their first event, the crew's preparation for the 1999 season was more carefully planned. Cracknell upped the tempo yet another notch. Coode noted that James worked hardest of the crew. 'You always think you've done a hard day's training until you've spent some time with him,' he said. 'That's when you realise you had been on a holiday beforehand.'

'Last year [1998], the response of the press to our defeat amazed me,' diarised Cracknell, 'showing how much any crew with Steve and Matt in it was expected to win. That is something you do not realise until you lose, which up until that point we hadn't. Losing last year gave me an insight into the downside of being a full-time athlete. This was my first loss since going full-time and, with no job or university forcing me to think about something else, it was a nightmare. Surprisingly, even the Playstation and MTV lost their appeal. In the build-up to the first World Cup regatta this was a feeling I was determined not to have again.'

The rowing world was puzzled to see the four in action, but with Coode on board and Foster in the single scull. Word went round. 'When is Tim coming back in?' . . . 'Is Tim going to get back in?'

In the single scull, Foster led his heat until the final 200 metres, when he faded during the sprint for the line. He surprised everyone with his time. Only four British scullers had ever sculled 2000 metres in under seven minutes. Foster's time was 7 minutes 0.4 seconds in non-fast conditions.

The selectors had a dilemma. Foster was back, but where

Luka Grubor had failed to mesh with the four, Coode fitted in seamlessly. The four glided to victory in their event, albeit against weak opposition – so weak that the Poles finished second. Coode walked the walk, talked the talk and rowed the row. Cracknell noted that, whereas he, Cracknell, was a nightmare-scenario man who throve on fear, Coode was unfazed by anything; he preserved his blood-and-soil Cornish nationalism on a nerveless block of ice. 'He'd make a great poker player,' said Cracknell.

Grobler could afford to keep Foster dangling, and both Grobler and Foster knew it.

The following week, Foster was slotted into the 7 seat of the British eight. Foster chafed at this outrage. In British rowing, top-rated oarsmen traditionally grace small boats, pairs and fours. The eight is low-status grunt work for embittered near-cast-offs and second-raters destined to sink to international rowing's lower tiers. Little was expected of this particular crew. In the previous year's World Championships (1998), they'd finished eighth. A similar result at the 1999 World Championships at St Catherine's in Canada would mean instant non-qualification for the Olympics, which demanded a finishing position no lower than seventh. Instant non-qualification! Having gone through what Foster had gone through, there was no way he was going to take this lying down. He felt 'relegated'. Stewing in an eight, you couldn't *shine*. Seven years after he thought he'd escaped the eight once and for all, there he was, a lowly galley slave once more. It was like starting over.

Foster made his displeasure known to Grobler. 'The eight is a nice alternative – to the single scull,' he fumed. 'But I haven't fought back from an operation, gone through hell and regained fitness only to be put in a boat that on present form doesn't even look like making it to Sydney.' Why was he cast in the eight at all? If fit for the eight, why not the four? What was Grobler's game? Worse still, his 'crew-mates' in the four were shunning him again. It was as if he was radioactive. 'The relationship had vanished,' he said. 'When we were rowing as a four, we got on very well. There was banter. We were definitely a four. When I wasn't in the four, *I definitely wasn't in the four.*'

Foster knew all too well the scale of the task ahead. It was more than just handbags. Coode, larger, heavier, stronger, enjoyed a full set of discs, but Foster was '90 per cent sure' he could do what was required to oust him. 'If Jürgen asked for a maximum squat test between me and Ed, I wouldn't be confident, but I'd be stupid enough to try.' *If I don't regain my seat this year*, he thought with indestructible optimism, *I'll ask how I can come back stronger next year. And if I don't get that chance, I'll ... go away and sulk for thirty years.*

The squad returned to Leander to prepare for the remainder of the summer regatta season, culminating in the World Championships in St Catherine's. Winter health niggles and weather worries gave way to fresh challenges, anglers pelting them with maggots, and the erratic steering of pleasure boats whose wash would sluice over the four's low-sided cut-away go-faster boat.

'Imagine the England football team training at Bisham Abbey with people jogging and walking their dogs on the pitch as David Beckham is lining up a practice free kick,' grumbled Cracknell in his diary.

In the eight, Foster found himself cast as the 'ancient mariner', a veteran of nine World Championships and two Olympic regattas. While he bored his crew-mates rigid with tales of the 1989 bronze-medal-winning eight, they would reply by telling him how they were still in short trousers at the time. Rowing in an eight is like a sustained sprint. It cruises at close to its maximum speed throughout a race. If you make a mistake or lose concentration, there is little time in which to recover and catch up. Fractions of a second often cover all the medallists. This makes eights exciting to watch but a mental and physical trial for rowers.

At Henley Royal Regatta in early July, the eight lost to the German national eight by half a length. The following weekend, the crew travelled to Lucerne, where every July the second largest international regatta (second to the World Championships) takes place on the Rotsee, God's gift to rowing, a lake hemmed in a deep crease in the Alps that is exactly 2000 metres long and six lanes wide and shielded from crosswinds. In their heat, the eight shot out like a Swiss cuckoo clock, and surprised many people, including themselves, by covering the course in the fastest time ever for a British eight over 2000 metres. In the final, they stormed from last at halfway to finish second, just three feet behind the winning Russian eight.

The four, meanwhile, got a scare from a slithery Norwegian crew who had spent several weeks of the previous winter cross-country skiing in the Italian Alps, and who had set a new world record in their heat. In the final, Norway attacked after 750 metres, and attacked again. At one point, just before the line, they even squeezed their bows in front, until the British four took the rate up to 46 strokes per minute to win by a canvas. 'Pinsent is the most powerful rower I've ever sat behind,' said Coode afterwards. 'Even at the end of a hard race, he can produce something extraordinary.'

Norway received a standing ovation for finishing second. They scented victory. 'Redgrave is getting older every week, and we have yet to reach our potential,' said Steffan Storseth of the Norwegian four. 'But the British four will not win in Sydney. We will be faster.'

Redgrave was quick to calm supporters' nerves. 'We knew they couldn't last the distance and they didn't,' he soothed. 'We had another couple of gears we didn't have to use.'

Grobler declared that he would announce the coxless four for the World Championships in St Catherine's on the Wednesday following Lucerne. Foster had no idea if he was destined for altitude training with the four in Austria, or training camp in Cambridge with the eight. He knew to expect neither sentiment nor mercy.

'There's success both ways,' said Redgrave doing his almighty best to stay out of the debate. 'We're unbeaten with Tim, and now we're unbeaten with Ed. We're in a no-lose position.' Cracknell reckoned there was nothing in it between Foster and Coode. 'Comparisons with Italy and Australia, who have exactly the same crews as last year, suggest that the four was at least as fast.'

Grobler took Foster aside at Leander. *Here we go*, thought Foster, steeling himself. *If he tells me I'm not in the four, I'll refuse to row*.

They sat on a park bench on a balcony overlooking the Leander garden. Grobler asked Foster to switch off his 'Gold Fever' video camera. Then he asked Foster what he thought of the four.

'It could go faster,' replied Foster. 'I think it needs me.'

Grobler thought for a moment. 'OK. But I think the eight needs you more. You are a key player and I need to qualify the eight for the Olympics. The four will win anyway.'

This wasn't what Foster wanted to hear. The great thing about sport is that you win or lose and get what you deserve; but here he was embroiled in a selection debate. He was in a no-win situation, damned if he made the eight go fast ('The eight needs you') and damned if he slowed it down ('You're not fit').

'I think I deserve my place in the four.' He eyed Grobler. 'You have effectively admitted that I deserve my place, but now you are saying I can't have it back, yet. One of the things that drove me from the depths of despair and made me fight to recover from my injury is that I wanted to get back to being the oarsman that I once was. I've done that. In fact, I'm better than I was. Now you're telling me the goalposts have moved. Put me in a boat and I'll beat Ed Coode. Put me in the four and it would go faster. But now you're saying you don't need it to go faster.' Foster had not felt firmer moral high ground beneath his feet in years.

'Tim, please. I will even go on my knees. I say this not as coach of the coxless four, but as the coach of the whole team. British rowing needs you. Trust me. This year is this year. Next year is next year. You are still part of the four's squad.'

But Foster had already trusted him. The deal was that if he went through with his operation and regained fitness, he'd recover his seat. Foster had met his side of the bargain. It was Grobler's turn to front up. Yet Foster felt Grobler's sinuous wiles working on him. He was being confronted by a messy sub-optimal situation, but could understand Grobler's argument and found himself being ineluctably won round.

'I'll let you know.'

Foster drove back to Oxford, where he lived. His sitting room, which was being rewired, was stripped bare of everything except his orthopaedic rocking chair designed to support bad backs. He sat rocking backwards and forwards on his own for three hours with the telephone on his lap, rotating his options in his mind. Foster could do one of three things: he could be selfless and row in the eight; or he could be selfish and appeal; or he could be stupid and refuse to row. Every few minutes, he'd pick up the receiver, begin to dial Grobler's number, then stop and put the receiver down. He was enjoined to silence by Grobler, so couldn't consult anyone from within the rowing world; nor was it worth asking anyone outside rowing, because their views would be largely irrelevant. He decided to flick on the video camera. He knew that anything he said to camera would not be broadcast until this present drama was water under Henley Bridge or over Hambleden Weir, so for two hours he talked to the red light on top of the camera, as if it were a silent friend. Finally he rang Grobler.

'Jürgen, I have decided to row in the eight at the World Championships.'

Wednesday, 14 July

A press conference was arranged at London Rowing Club at Putney. The kit said it all. Pinsent, Redgrave, Cracknell and Coode arrived in Lycra shorts and sweatshirts; Foster sported blue damask trousers and shiny buckled shoes. It was not an easy decision, said Grobler, but he had two principal considerations. 'First, never change a successful crew, and secondly, if we can win with a new guy, that's a bonus. Foster and Coode will be part of the fours squad for the Olympic year.'

So that was it. Foster, previously the 'fourth man', was now the 'fifth Beatle', frozen out of the Fab Four. That he appeared to make the eight go very fast indeed only seemed to count against his aspirations towards the four, especially as Coode was getting along so well in that boat.

'I am very disappointed,' he said. 'It's been difficult watching a crew I see as my own from the outside. I told Jürgen at the beginning of the season that I haven't gone through everything I've gone through in rowing to race in the eight, but Lucerne helped me change my mind. I don't know what they think about having this old man in the middle of them, but my role in this eight is something I can be positive about. No one expects the eight to win. The fact that promise has come out of the blue makes it a different challenge.'

Coode kept a low profile. 'I didn't realise the decisions would take so long,' he said. 'Up to Lucerne, I just concentrated on the race. It was the closest one all season, and afterwards I kept wondering if I'd done my best.'

Another aspect of rowing in an eight is the logistical challenge of transporting, accommodating and feeding eight oarsmen. It turned out that the eight's Cambridge training camp hadn't yet been fully organised, so Foster effectively took charge. Hitting the telephones at the ARA's headquarters in Hammersmith, he located a likely-looking hotel near Ely, established whether it could take a crew of eight oarsmen, then faxed over dietary details. Meanwhile, Foster's mother was on standby to help with the cooking if required. Foster also took over the inboard coaching of the eight. At first the boat didn't go particularly well. Foster thought that the crew should pick up the catch quicker. During easy-all lulls, he would talk into the cox's microphone so that his words were relayed throughout the boat.

This began to irk Martin McElroy, the coach of the eight, a volatile character who was known not to hit it off with Grobler. He began to suspect that Foster was part of some bigger scheme of Grobler's to wrest power from his hands.

'I valued Martin and obeyed him as much as I did Jürgen,' says Foster. 'I thought it was best to be open to Martin and the rest of the crew, and that if I were open and honest they'd appreciate it.'

McElroy soon began to feel his territory was being invaded. The tension began to build. Finally, bristling, he called the crew together after an outing. 'We can either do things my way,' he said in his tethered voice, 'or you can eff off.' His words, although directed at the crew in general, were aimed at Foster. McElroy was soon calmed down by the crew. The following day, Robin Williams, chief rowing coach of Cambridge University, watched the crew rowing.

'What you guys need to work on is the catch.'

Foster smiled. McElroy was much easier to handle after

that. He realised Foster's comments were positive and not part of a power play.

St Catherine's is located in the south-west portion of the province of Ontario, amid the Niagara Peninsular fruit belt, twelve miles from the US border. The World Championship regatta was to take place in the high-banked Martindale Pond, where the annual Royal Canadian Henley Regatta takes place.

In the coxless fours, the feisty Norwegians seemed to have believed their own publicity, because they finished fifth in the final, six seconds down on Great Britain, who won in a stupendous row. 'Simply awesome,' said Redgrave afterwards. 'We went for complete control and got it. We didn't let anyone back in and it felt easy.' Pinsent thought the final was his best championship race ever.

The coxless four, 'my boat' (Foster), was now a proven World-Championship-winning outfit. It hadn't just edged the title. It had cruised it. When Foster had been in the coxless four, he, Pinsent and Redgrave had stood head and shoulders above any other oarsmen in the British squad. Now Coode was up there too. A betting man would have put his shirt on Coode retaining his seat.

It was Foster's move. Besides himself, no one from the eight had ever won a World Championship medal. Foster told them how to do it. He gathered the crew around him and gave them the fifteen-minute pep talk of their lives.

'The level of training among all the crews is so similar and the difference in physical performance is so minute that the difference between each crew is in the mental application and the ability to keep a clear head and yet still push yourself through the pain barrier. You have to get yourself in a position where you give yourself a chance to succeed. When that opportunity arises, you must have your wits about you to seize it. When your legs are screaming, when your heart is racing at almost 200 beats a minute, and the last thing you want to do is reach out for another stroke, you have to keep going. If you do, and you stand on that medal rostrum, it won't hurt. Promise.'

Great Britain drew lane six, alongside joint favourites Russia and the USA, who had won the eights title for the previous two years. After a furious first 500 metres, the USA and Britain were both out in front and racing stroke for stroke, with Russia trailing. The crews held their positions until, with 600 metres to go, the British eight raised the rate to 38 and squeezed their bows in front. This triggered a dash for the line, in which the USA clocked a last 500 metres fully three seconds faster than Great Britain's to win by just over a second. It was a storming row, and it qualified the British eight for the Sydney Olympics.

As they paddled, gulping down lungfuls of air, to the landing stage, Grobler was throwing bodies out of the way to be the first to congratulate Foster. He grabbed Foster's hand, squeezed it with an iron grip, and pulled him into a great bear hug.

It was a terrific performance by the crew, the finest by a British heavyweight men's eight since 1981 – so terrific that there was almost a twinge of frustration that they hadn't hung on to snatch Britain's first gold in an eight since 1912.

'The crew believed me when I said it wouldn't hurt,' said Foster. 'Having stood on that medal rostrum, they knew I was lying because it hurts like hell, but it feels good too.'

Once again, behind the rostrum smiles, frustration gnawed. How could Foster expect Grobler to disrupt the four and the eight when both were going so well? 'I've helped qualify the eight for the Olympics,' he said, 'but I want to row in the top boat and that looks like being the coxless four.'

This was not so much a problem as another challenge to overcome.

10

Olympic Year

23 September 1999

The squad reconvened for the final 'Olympic season'. The banter dropped off. The haggling over how far they rowed each day stopped (not that it had ever achieved much). The moaning about training died down. Muscles swung to their familiar task. Grobler brought zero-tolerance to hazardous extracurricular activities, skiing, rugby and motorcycling. He was not amused when Pinsent failed to turn up for the first two days.

After two days' training at Henley, the squad flew to Australia bound for the British Olympic Association training camp on the Gold Coast, where a three-week camp would test the facilities for the pre-Games build-up the following year. The squad pored over Grobler's programme of football, weights, rowing, 'beach games' and cycling. 'Beach games' turned out to be long-distance runs on the beach. Cycling was conducted with police outriders baffled at why the squad kept insisting on cycling up the largest hill in the area. The day's training over, the biggest challenge was staying awake for the Rugby Union World Cup then taking place in France.

Officially, the slate was wiped clean. The squad would be assessed anew. The coxless four would remain the top-rated crew. Three of the seats were already booked. The fourth seat read, 'Coode or Foster?' Its ultimate occupant would be settled by a straight shoot-out: Foster versus Coode; Cornish cream versus Great Ouse charm; big biceps versus big hair; Etonian drawl versus Bedford twang; clean-cut kite-flyer versus Heavy Metal dandy; West Country Goliath versus East Anglian David. Over the next six months, Grobler would call the shots at his leisure. First, he would have some fun. He put down Foster and Coode as room-mates in Australia (you could always tell how well you were doing within the squad by whoever Grobler appointed as your room-mate). 'Would you like boxing gloves to settle it here and now?' he laughed.

One day, Grobler asked to see Foster in private. They sat on a sofa in a hallway adjacent to the entrance to the dining room in their Gold Coast hotel. 'So Tim, last but not least, I'd like to say, without using big words . . . you know me, I use short words . . .' as usual it took Grobler two minutes to get to the point '. . . I'd like to say that this year will be a tough one. We will have to train harder and go faster . . .' Cutting to the quick, without telling Foster in so many words that he was back in the four, he seemed to refer to it obliquely when he suggested that Foster had the right qualities and that these could come in handy '. . . and I mean Ed is a World Champion and we can't drop him just yet.'

Monday, 18 October

Back at the Hellespont, Pinsent, in earnest of hard work, arrived one morning with a cube-shaped digital alarm clock that he plugged into a power point in the Leander boathouse. He set it to ring at 8.15 a.m. If you weren't on the water by then, it was noted. Every morning the crew would stand around, waiting for it to go off, then leap into action.

Various tests were hurled at the squad to decide the final seating order before the summer regatta season, which began in May 2000. Coode and Foster trained shoulder-to-shoulder, ergometer-machine-to-ergometer-machine at the Leander Club, while checking the sky for smoke signals from Grobler.

Although they both coveted the same seat, Foster and Coode got along remarkably well, considering what was at stake. 'I hold nothing against Ed,' said Foster. 'It's weird that he watched videos of me. I respect him. He improved a lot last year. He trains well. In purely physical terms, he can do things that I cannot. Today we did a 16 kilometre ergometer. He finished two minutes ahead of me. We did a maximum weights test. Ed was going for a final lift on bench press. I said, "Go on, Ed." I was surprised – and pleased – that he only managed 90 kilograms to my 105 (Pinsent's maximum was about 135 kilograms). Without me being malicious, it was good for me to beat him. If I can use me-vs-Ed to better myself, I can create something positive from it. It was jolly lucky too for Ed that he was competing against me and not, say, Greg Searle.'

Foster's ace was always his technique and 'boat-moving abilities'. In a single sculling boat – the purest test of skill over muscle – he left the squad for dead. He grew unto his seat; the oars and shell became as it were part of his central nervous system. He regularly outstripped Pinsent during day-to-day training. Over 1000 metres, he'd put ten seconds on Ed Coode.

On board, he was the Sorcerer – catalyst, facilitator and translator of his crew-mates' power. He made those around him row better; when he'd been in the four, he'd allowed Pinsent and Redgrave to lengthen their strokes. As onboard coach, he was a great talker during and after an outing.

'Coaches can see, but not feel,' he said. 'I have a good feel for the run of a boat. If something doesn't feel right, I'll say so. That's what I bring to the four. I must beat Ed at everything possible, so that whatever selection criteria are used, I am better than him. But what favours me is the way the boat runs . . .

'On a rowing machine, weight is an advantage. In a boat it is a disadvantage. You have to carry that weight. Add 10 kilograms to a crew, and the boat will sit lower in the water, increasing its drag. My light weight shows up on the ergo. But in a boat, I don't have that disadvantage. In fact, I have an advantage. Were Ed and I of equal standard, you'd choose the more reliable body. In that way, I'm more of a risk. But I haven't seen anything in the boat that I can't improve on.'

The squad's first engagement was in November 1999 at the Fours Head of the River at Putney. Foster sculled in a 'quad' with Cracknell, fellow squad member Bobby Thatcher and Ed Coode. They won, but as the Fours Head is, like the Eights Head of the River Race, largely a PR exercise for the squad, little was read into the result.

In December, a timed sculling trial took place under louring skies and lashing winds at the *ultima Thule* of Boston. Just beforehand, Foster accidentally slashed his hand and sculled badly bloodied. He finished joint second with Pinsent. Coode won. Grobler agreed the result was a blip and told Foster not to worry.

Meanwhile, health and injury scares haunted the squad once again. At about this time, Cracknell contracted a strain of glandular fever, but managed to hush it up. His white-blood-cell count shot up and his training suffered as his body fought the virus. 'It was incredibly worrying,' he says. 'Had it lasted longer than February, it would have been a much bigger issue. I'm not Steve Redgrave. They weren't going to wait for someone like me. I didn't feel on top form until March. I found it really hard to share the pressure, to tell people what I was feeling.'

'Well hang on,' said Foster. 'My impression was that, because James had never had a winter virus before, it assumed larger proportions for him than for the rest of us. Personally I was never worried that he wouldn't recover. He may say he wasn't on top form until March, but he was still pulling personal bests on the ergo.'

In January, Redgrave, playing about on a physio ball, fell off and hurt his arm, but carried on training. 'Just another knock to add to all the others I've taken in a career at the top spanning four decades ...' The next day, still in pain, he checked into hospital and found he'd fractured his forearm. The bad news was that he was off training for six weeks. The good news was that he would miss the pairs trial that Grobler had scheduled at Boston in February. Redgrave's bench presses were never the same after that.

February 2000

It was back to Boston yet again for a timed pairs trial. Foster and Cracknell won. Coode and Greg Searle finished third. More encouraging still – for Foster – Coode and Searle were beaten by Bobby Thatcher and Steve Trapmore, who were down to row in the eight and were not considered pair aspirants. This was surely Grobler's cue to favour Foster. But he delayed. The theory rippled through the squad that the 'right' result hadn't been achieved – 'right' in the sense of 'right' for Grobler. Searle had been struggling in the single scull. In fact, his three years in the toughest trade in the sport had seen him slump from third in the world in 1997 to fourteenth in 1999, eliminating him from the Olympic single sculls at Sydney. He was a far superior rower than sculler. The obvious solution was to pair Searle with the 'loser' of Coode vs Foster; but the Boston result showed that Coode and Searle needed more development. The best way of putting a rocket under the pair's performance was to keep the Foster/Coode situation as unstable as possible, and while you're about it, keep Searle hanging out to dry.

Monday, 21 February 2000

An as yet unresolved squad headed for training camp in Seville with the coxless four looking as overbooked as an asylum seeker's fishing boat. This camp had a twist: seat-racing. Seat-racing is a way of comparing one oarsman against another. Take a boat or two, and a pool of oarsmen. Shuffle the oarsmen among each boat and make them race against each other in different combinations or against the clock, in order to sift prime movers from boat-stoppers. It is not a fail-safe test, since it assumes neutrality on the part of all crew members and that they are all doing their damnedest. In this series of seat races, Redgrave and Pinsent stayed fixed in the boat, while they were joined alternately by Foster, Cracknell, Coode and Searle. They raced four times over 1500 metres with different combinations. It emerged that, on stroke side, Cracknell was better than Searle, which boosted his confidence, while on bow side, Foster edged Coode. Foster in fact won every race he rowed in (among Foster's remarkable achievements, he cannot remember ever having lost a seat race). However many times and in whichever way Grobler shuffled the deck, Foster came up trumps. 'Whichever way you looked at it,' he says, 'the boat was faster with me.'

'But having said that,' wrote Redgrave in his autobiography *A Golden Age*, 'we had one outing in the second week in Seville with Ed, and it was probably the best session we'd ever had. I honestly don't know which was the best four, and thankfully it was not my decision.'

Grobler called a squad meeting and, without using big words, dilated for half an hour without once mentioning crew selection. His motive soon became clear. Bolted on to this Seville training camp was a FISA Team Cup regatta and the Andalusia regatta, two close-season invitation-only fixtures held over the same weekend for crews from Denmark – including the slippery Danish lightweight four – Germany and Holland. Grobler coveted the Victor Ludorum. He reckoned the coxless four would win irrespective of whether Coode or Foster was on board. However, spurred by a perverse desire to beat his German compatriots, Grobler also wanted to win the pairs. Since Foster made a pair go faster than Coode, Grobler – for the purpose of this one-off event – was minded to slot Foster into the pair and Coode into the four.

On the Saturday, the four, Foster up, raced the Danes over 1000 metres and won 'quite comfortably' (Redgrave). Coode and Searle lost to a German pair. That annoyed Grobler. On the Sunday, the four were due to race the Danes again. Grobler wanted to swap Foster with Coode. The four protested that a loss would send out the wrong message to opponents. Cracknell got dead vocal on the issue.

Frustration bubbled over. Redgrave began to throw snide comments at Grobler, deliberately directed short, sharp prods ('So we're a bunch of amateurs, are we?') and petulant remarks about the coaching, which wouldn't normally get a rise out of Grobler. But nothing Grobler could do was right. At the back of Redgrave's mind lurked a sense that the coxless four was being held up by matters beyond his control, namely Grobler's opaque agenda. For Foster, the situation echoed the previous summer, when his talents and prospects were being sacrificed 'to help out other crews'. Redgrave would not be trifled with. He took Grobler aside and told him there was no guarantee that the four, with Coode up, would win, especially as Grobler was continually chopping and changing the seating order. The Olympics were just seven months away, and here he was tinkering with the crew to win meaningless events at inconsequential close-season invitation regattas: so inconsequential that not even Foster's parents – the most loyal, most supportive parents within the squad – had bothered to turn up. This was the tensest exchange between Grobler and the squad. Redgrave had never rowed in an Olympic crew selected so late.

'Steve and Matthew had been told the four would be decided before Christmas,' says Foster. 'Then they were promised a decision before Seville. They were prepared to concede a couple of months, but that was all. They were gagging to get started. Steve told me he was surprised Jürgen hadn't asked him about crew selection. Normally, Grobler consulted people. This time, however, he was definitely keeping shtum and being deliberate vague.'

Grobler backed down. Foster stayed on board – for the moment at least. The four won. Coode and Searle lost – to a different German pair. That annoyed Grobler even more.

At the end of Seville, nothing was committed. 'I was looking at the results and thinking that not even the most biased observer could possibly construe these results in any way other than favouring me,' says Foster. 'I was happy with how things had gone on the water. The only drawback was that Seville was not a formal trial, but a one-off regatta. I'd convinced myself that the reason for Grobler's delay was to extract a good result from Greg and Ed. Yes, that was it. Jürgen wanted whoever missed out on the four to have something positive to go into.'

Thursday, 23 March 2000

As the squad returned home, Grobler had it in writing that Foster made a boat go faster than Coode. He declared that the final selection would be announced at the ARA regatta at Holmepierrepoint watersports centre in Nottingham in April. Meanwhile there was the matter of the 2000 metre ergometer test to sort out.

The Concept II ergometer rowing machine is accepted worldwide as the definitive measure of an oarsman's physical capability. He sits on a sliding seat and pulls a handle attached to a bicycle chain, which drives a flywheel. Cracknell once described an ergometer machine as giving 'a very accurate feeling of all the bad things about rowing, the pain, the repetitiveness and frustration, but none of the good things, like the feeling of the boat moving beneath you, the sense of speed, relaxation, enjoyment and fulfilment'.

Rob Waddell, the New Zealand sculler, held the world record over 2000 metres with a time of 5 minutes 39.5 seconds. Redgrave's best time was 5 minutes 46 seconds, set in 1997. What the ergo cannot replicate is the racing shell's acute sensitivity to rhythm, balance and momentum. It therefore hides a multitude of technical rowing sins and favours the fit and the powerful over the technically gifted. Talented underweights like Foster were bound to underperform.

Whereas all the squad relished racing in boats at regattas, several of them dreaded the ergometer test. It wasn't like the strength test at the British Olympic Association Medical Centre, which simply measured how you'd adapted nature's endowment. The ergo tested your character too. There was no end to the exquisite and excruciating pain it provided, and it was therefore a very real measurable test of how hard you could push yourself. Some squad members felt they had to achieve things above and beyond what they were capable of in a boat; they generally fared poorest. Those who fared best treated it like any old race, as something to be savoured, not psyched out by. 'If you race the distance rather than let the machine get on top of you,' said Cracknell, 'I find they go much quicker. Imagine yourself rowing down a course with the markers going past and what you should be doing at each marker.'

For days beforehand, the squad discussed likely outcomes. The consensus emerged that Pinsent could easily break the world record – if he could be bothered – with Cracknell finishing second and Redgrave third.

That morning, excepting a few absentees, twenty-four oarsmen presented themselves at the Leander gym, stringently braced for action, along with an audience of about thirty others come to soak up the atmosphere and enjoy the spectacle. Ergometer test day was family entertainment at its finest. The shrieking of the ergometers, the droplets of sweat on the floor, the anguished 'oh no!' expressions on the oarsmen's faces, the bulging eyeballs glued to the computerised monitors as if lives depended on them, and then the final physical collapse at the end all amounted to quite an event. Grobler always wore a tricoteuse's smile on ergo test day.

Before the tests began, each oarsman warmed up over 12 kilometres, which took between forty-five and fifty minutes. Then, working in groups of three, the men would await their turn, step forward, sit on the machine, strap themselves in and row 2000 metres flat out. It is almost frowned upon within the squad not to embarrass yourself at the end of an ergometer test, so after completing 2000 metres, which takes just under six minutes, each oarsman would literally have to be peeled off the sweat-drenched floor, while three fresh contenders were pushed forward. Ergo tests had all the thrill of a public execution, but with fewer casualties.

At 10 a.m., Redgrave, Pinsent and Cracknell addressed the three ergometers lined up alongside each other. A hush descended. For Redgrave, this would his last full-battledress setpiece competitive ergo test in an international rowing career spanning twenty-one years. Foster and Cracknell noted how uptight he'd seemed beforehand, how anxious he was to put up a good valedictory time that would go down in the annals of rowing. His outstanding performances in training suggested he was at least up for a personal best.

They blasted off in unison, Cracknell at an insane pace, which he struggled to keep up. Pinsent soon found his racing pace and rowed through Cracknell; but Cracknell was giving it everything, and more. With 250 metres to go, his face, twisted with monstrous lineaments, had turned white, his skin appeared to have shrink-wrapped itself around his skull, and his lips had turned Oxford blue. But it was Pinsent's day. Matthew finished in a phenomenal time of 5 minutes 42 seconds, the second fastest time over 2000 metres ever recorded. Cracknell smashed his personal best with 5 minutes 46.9 seconds.

Among Redgrave's strengths was his explosive power off the start which often destroyed the opposition psychologically. Unfortunately, ergometer machines don't have psyches. He went off hard and kept up a blistering pace for two minutes, and then . . . began to slow . . . and . . . cracked. He died on the machine. But no way was Redgrave, being Redgrave, going to stop. He limped on.

'I've never known Steve stop on an ergo,' says Foster. 'He's too stubborn.'

Redgrave's time – 6 minutes 10 seconds – was a shocker, the slowest of the day. His cracking up was less a sign of his being unfit, than of his believing himself fitter than he was. Or, it might have been an 'off' day such as diabetes and colitis tended to bring. Grobler, Pinsent and Foster unpeeled him from the ergometer and waited for him to begin breathing again.

His confidence was badly knocked. He and Grobler later had words.

As for Pinsent, he'd just missed out on the world record, but how hard had he tried? Twenty-five seconds after recording the second-fastest time in history, there he was leaping up like a jack-in-the-box to help catch Redgrave. Had Pinsent had Cracknell's drive, one wonders how far he could have gone. Had he genuinely fulfilled his potential? Cracknell would discuss this with Foster at a later date – several later dates in fact.

Foster came in sixth in 5 minutes 53.4 seconds, 1.5 seconds off his personal best. Coode had gone before Redgrave, Pinsent and Cracknell, but had cracked after 1000 metres. Once you've cracked doing a competitive ergo, there's no way back. It's not a question of having a breather and beginning again. That's it. You've blown it. Two weeks later Coode re-sat and timed 5 minutes 53.5 seconds – 0.1 seconds slower than Foster. Foster magnanimously downplayed the significance of the result, describing himself as 'pretty happy'. 'Besides,' he said, 'my strengths lie in things the ergo doesn't show.'

The squad split into pairs – Redgrave and Pinsent, Cracknell and Foster, and Coode and Searle – and turned their attention to the ARA pairs trial regatta at Holmepierrepoint the following month.

A few days after the ergo test, the six top athletes in the squad met Grobler at the Leander Club to discuss how best to prepare for the pairs trial. Foster and Cracknell sensed a brooding, faintly threatening silence emanating from Redgrave, while nimbuses consulted above him.

Cracknell and Searle piped up by saying that all three pairs should work together. This was the sort of warm, feel-good, consensual option that Redgrave would instantly react against.

'No,' he grunted. 'This is a race. We're three separate pairs, and it's about which one is fastest.'

For the next three weeks, there was no question of Pinsent and Redgrave hanging around the Leander boat bays waiting for Pinsent's alarm clock to go off and scrambling Le Mans-style. They turned up earlier than any other pair and would have finished three training sessions before Cracknell and Foster had even completed two. They made a point of not necessarily co-operating with the rest of the squad, 'Not in a nasty way,' recalls Greg Searle. 'It reminded me I wasn't there to help them. I was rowing against them ... In many ways, there's more to lose in these races than in an international regatta. These are proud guys and there's a lot of rivalry between Steve and Matt, and Tim and James, and a lot at stake for everyone.'

Redgrave's body language and abruptness seemed to confirm what Foster and Cracknell were witnessing on the water: that Pinsent and Redgrave's pair was going like a bucket and that Matt and Steve were beginning to fret. Redgrave had come out fighting in a manner that the others hadn't expected. They were offering him the group, whereas Redgrave was getting ready to go off in a sulk and fight it out for himself. He was making it more of a challenge than it needed to be. A rift was emerging. Cracknell and Foster saw theirs as the way forward; Pinsent and Redgrave thought otherwise. They'd all performed the same training, but, by concentrating on quality, Cracknell and Foster had extracted more from it than Pinsent and Redgrave, who had merely *got the training done*, rushing through it while leaving 'something in hand'. Redgrave and Pinsent, meanwhile, thought Foster and Cracknell were faffing about.

'Had you asked Matthew to do a 40 kilometre ergo, he'd try and do it in one session,' says Foster. 'Ask James, and he'd split it into three chunks and give every kilometre the respect it deserved. The ideal may be somewhere between the two approaches. Steve and Matthew, who were experienced winners, believed that work done ultimately delivered results. But basic technical flaws were slowing them down. They were rowing with short and muscular strokes, rather than long efficient ones – great for killing fish and terrorising ducks, but useless for moving boats. They were jabbing the blade in at the catch and ripping through the water, rather than levering the boat past the spoon of the oar, which is the desired effect. Their "puddles" were big and frothy, rather than solid and small. They were falling back on their strengths, not addressing their weaknesses.'

Redgrave knew that this impending trial would be tribulation to him, less a chance to stamp his authority on the squad than a duck shoot aimed at his reputation. He was even less amused that the trial would be attended by the world's media.

'That must have been a very strange feeling for Redgrave, going into the pairs trial knowing he would lose,' mused Foster, who craved winning the trial almost more than being selected for the four.

He and Cracknell had targeted this fixture ever since Christmas. Cracknell was licking his lips in anticipation of beating Redgrave and Pinsent. 'The satisfaction gained from beating the best pair in history will be immeasurable,' he drooled in his diary in the *Daily Telegraph*. Foster was less confident. He worried that his and Cracknell's superiority in training would merely goad Pinsent and Redgrave to greater things in the trials.

On the eve of the regatta, Pinsent went to see the physiotherapist about a back niggle. *Oh yes, here we go*, thought Cracknell, interpreting Pinsent's move as laying the foundations for a tactical withdrawal. The rest of the squad even began placing bets as to whether Redgrave and Pinsent would pull out or not.

'No matter how bad Matthew's back is, it can't be worse than mine,' Foster told Cracknell.

Cracknell shot back a worried look. 'Your back? How bad is it?'

'No worse than normal,' shrugged Foster, simulating a convincing wince.

11 April 2000

The dank nihilism of Holmepierrepoint is exceeded only by that of the big ditch at Boston. A featureless, blasted, oblong, concrete lake with an air of desertion about it, this was the unlikely, unglamorous setting for the final showdown, the ARA pairs trials: twenty-two oarsmen would compete for four-teen Olympic places in the eight, the coxless four and coxless pair. No doubt Grobler had already decided on what he'd decide, but Jürgen's paperwork was always outstanding, and the rubber-stamp formalities of such occasions were all part of his professionalism. Afterwards, Grobler would have no choice but to show his hand and announce the full and final seating arrangements for the Olympic party.

The two-day regatta consisted of a 2000 metre time trial on the Tuesday morning followed by a semi-final in the after-noon. The final would be held the following morning. The media locked on to the three-way shoot-out between Red-grave and Pinsent, Foster and Cracknell and Coode and Searle – not that the television crews and photographers could see much, peering into Holmepierrepoint's subfusc gloom.

In the time trial, Foster and Cracknell won by 0.2 seconds over Coode and Searle. Redgrave and Pinsent came nowhere. That afternoon Foster and Cracknell won their semi-final with insolent ease. They were four or five lengths up at halfway and by the end were patronising the opposition by rating a lowly 25 strokes a minute.

The following morning, in the final, six pairs stormed away in good flat water. After 1500 metres Foster and Cracknell were two lengths up on the field. For most of the race, Pinsent and Redgrave lay fifth, having a ghastly blood-and-guts row. 'So much harder than any race I've ever done,' said Redgrave afterwards. It looked as if their glorious partnership as a pair would end in humiliation. In the neighbouring lane, Louis

Attrill and Andrew Lindsay, who were rowing in the eight, were thinking the unthinkable: that they might beat the greatest pair of all time. Meanwhile David Tanner, the British rowing team manager, was wondering how he was going to explain such a poor show to a press already sensing unease within the squad.

With 250 metres to go, a cry went up from Redgrave, 'Three tens!' Within fifteen seconds, Attrill and Lindsay were rowing in Pinsent and Redgrave's wash as, shutting their eyes and taking a deep breath, they sprinted the last few metres home, clawing their way up to third place, just behind Coode and Searle. This was Redgrave and Pinsent's first defeat in side-by-side racing in years, and would be their last race in a pair.

'It just didn't click any more,' reflected Pinsent. 'But we could have finished fifth in that race, which would have opened us up to attack from others in the squad. This makes Jürgen's job easier. It's a new thing for Steve to be beaten by his own countrymen in his own country, but I'm not too worried about him. He's handing over to a new generation, and it's good to do that now, not after he's finished.'

Redgrave spun the result cleverly. 'We've been playing catch-up,' he said. 'But don't forget that, last time we lost a selection trial here in 1992, the pair that beat us went on to win Olympic gold (the Searle brothers) and so did we. I'd say I've had my best winter since Atlanta.'

After the race Foster rang his mother with the news. 'I owe her an awful lot,' he said.

Grobler was thrilled. His three pairs – his personal charges – had finished as the top three. His plan had been to tease out of Coode vs Foster a coxless four and a pair worthy of Olympic gold. Now Coode and Searle were coming good. He could safely drop Coode from the four and parachute him into a pair with genuine gold-medal form, without crushing Coode's ego – not that Coode's ego was especially fragile, but Grobler had paternal instincts towards the younger members of the squad.

'This is the cuddly side of Jürgen,' says Foster. 'He cares about his athletes in that way. I'm sure the reason Ed was not dropped straight away was because Jürgen wanted him to get into the next best boat, i.e. the pair. He doesn't enjoy dropping people, especially not people like Ed, who contributed a lot to the four and had many skills to offer.'

Foster and Cracknell's demolition of Pinsent and Redgrave was in a way momentous. It heralded a new pecking order within the squad. They were showing Pinsent and Redgrave the way. The 'other two' had become 'the pair', and 'the pair' had become 'the other two'. Perhaps this result would serve as a lesson, Cracknell and Foster said to each other. 'Now we have at least as much a say as they do.'

The four had a meeting shortly afterwards. Cracknell was vocal about what had to be done, brimming with confidence. Foster, less vocal, was keen to get the four going. In practice, the pendulum took its time to swing in their favour. It wasn't as if the squad suddenly said, 'OK, we'll do things James and Tim's way.'

'We had confirmation that ours was the right way,' says Foster. 'James isn't necessarily a confident person, but this was a boost. He had nothing more to prove. His seat was safe. He'd championed his way and been vindicated. He had confidence that he was not only worth his place and was a fantastic athlete, but that his opinions were worthy too.'

Unknown to the crew at the time, Grobler was mentally shuffling the deck in other ways. He later admitted to Cracknell that, in the light of his and Foster's pairs bombshell, he was tempted to break up the four, keep Cracknell and Foster as a pair, and make a new four out of Searle, Coode, Pinsent and Redgrave (then watch it explode). 'He was convinced that the pair was the squad's best chance of gold,' says Foster. 'But

Jürgen wanted two shots at gold, which in his eyes meant keeping the Pinsent-Redgrave-Foster-Cracknell four and pairing Coode with Searle.'

That summer, Foster and Cracknell found that the old order had not been completely upended. Redgrave and Pinsent still hogged the belvedere room at Silvretta.

Grobler wasn't so worried about Redgrave and Pinsent's poor form. Redgrave, it was felt, was only capable of putting together two big races a year, and the April trial certainly hadn't been one of them. He was husbanding his resources. True, were you to look at Redgrave's performances in a critical light, he might not have broken into the squad at all. In the single scull he was way down the field. Pairing with Pinsent, he was nowhere. In Foster's opinion, there wasn't much between Cracknell and Pinsent as a pair's partner, but Redgrave was pairing with the highest-rated member of the squad in Pinsent, yet still going backwards.

Within the crew, however, there was nothing but a genuine belief that Redgrave had one final card to play in the soupy cauldron at Penrith. Foster never doubted it, not even when Redgrave was hard to distinguish from a list of symptoms and a well-developed self-belief. 'With Steve we have been in this situation before: he has had a better winter than in previous years. There has been no colitis and no diabetes as in 1997/8. He is his own harshest critic. If he felt he was in a boat purely because he was Steve Redgrave, he'd pull out. He'd drop himself, before Grobler got close. I don't think he'd do that now. I genuinely feel he wants to have to fight for himself. He has that package of determination, drive, will-to-win and bloody-mindedness that makes him stand out.

'In Jürgen's eyes there is the world of difference between a gold-medal standard athlete and a gold-medal-winning athlete. Steve has learnt to win and has taught Matthew how to win too. He has this singular performance in him, that is part of his character. James is driven, Steve is determined. Despite having done it four times before, Steve still has the will to push himself. I'd still prefer Steve next to me in the trenches than Ed. I'd agree with arguments about what Ed's done, but I'd prefer Steve.'

As for Pinsent, his rowing kit was looking increasingly snug. A great pack of muscle capable of tremendous leverage, Pinsent was the strongest man in the squad. At 115 kilograms, he was also the heaviest and it wasn't all muscle. He was still 'wearing his winter warmers', 7 to 8 kilos of excess blubber. The chocolate binges, takeaways and extemporised bachelor cooking were taking their toll. Dead weight drags a coxless four by about one second per 5 kilos over 2000 metres. Pinsent was slowing the boat down by some 1.5 seconds, or half a boat's length. That could be the difference between finishing first and finishing nowhere. Grobler took him to one side.

Foster had a quiet chat with Jacqueline Boorman, the Olympic rowing squad's official nutritionist. Grobler didn't entirely hold with modern sports scientists. He always told Foster he should weigh more and would feed him his pudding. He would occasionally tell Pinsent he was too heavy, and try to put the brakes on him. Otherwise, Grobler was old-fashioned in his approach to nutritional science. Foster, however, had worked with Boorman in the eight in 1999, and knew her value.

'It is a common misconception amongst rowers and coaches that bigger is better in rowing,' he says. 'This leads to phrases like, "It doesn't matter what I eat, I'll burn it off with my training," or just fat rowers. Whatever weight you are, you have to carry it in the boat.'

Boorman analysed the crew's diet. Each member was to record every mouthful they ate or drank for a week. She fed the audit into a computer, which regurgitated a breakdown of nutrients and calories. Cracknell and Foster recorded their intake scrupulously and were found to have excellent diets. They regarded their intake as fuelling an engine designed for a specific task. Pinsent, on the other hand, reckoned his engine was fine and didn't care what he shovelled into it. He certainly didn't lack basic nutrients. He breakfasted heartily on bacon sandwiches, or 'full English', his only concession to 'healthy' eating being poached, not fried, eggs.

'Jacqueline Boorman helped the four largely at mine and James's request,' says Foster. 'It was an elaborate ruse to get Pinsent to agree he was overweight. In the test, there was always a suspicion that he wasn't being entirely honest about his diet, or was simply forgetting what he ate.'

Thursday, 13 April 2000

Grobler told the four to arrive at Leander the following day at 8 a.m. for his official announcement, followed by a press conference at 10.30 a.m. He then departed the scene. Later that day, Redgrave picked up a message from Grobler telling him to be at Leander at 7.30 a.m. Wuh ... what did this mean? Why half an hour earlier than the others? He rang Cracknell. Nope, said Cracknell, Grobler had said 8 a.m. A frantic flurry of telephone calls ensued as Redgrave rang the others. They'd all been told 8 a.m. Redgrave's thoughts reeled. Was he about to be dropped in a quiet one-to-one with Grobler before the others turned up?

He spent a fretful night. Although he reckoned his seat was secure, his performance that year, if looked at dispassionately with the eyes of an East German coach with number-crunching propensities, suggested that he was the weakest link. His fractured forearm in January, the missed Boston pairs trial, the ergo debacle in March and the flunked selection regatta in April amounted to a litany of underperformance.

Surely it was his seat that was in doubt? Was Coode still in with a shout now as *his* supplanter?

What in fact had happened was that Grobler had rung all the squad members to revise the time, but only Redgrave had bothered to check his messages.

The rowing world eagerly awaited the announcement. Internet forums had been hanging on every move the squad made, partly because all the other top international squads had already announced their line-ups and were awaiting Great Britain's.

Friday, 14 April

Everyone reckoned they knew what the outcome of the meeting would be. As Cracknell said, 'The educated money was on the final combo even in March.' It took Grobler, never one to use a few long efficient words where many muscularly jabbed-in short ones would do (the similarities between Grobler's speech and Pinsent and Cracknell's pair were all too apparent), forty-five minutes actually to announce the crews. As he ran through Pinsent's performance, then Cracknell's, then Redgrave's ('I am very confident to have him in the crew based on his high performances'), doubts began to creep into Foster's mind, while his heart began to pound.

'If I'm not selected,' he thought, 'I'll throw my toys around and appeal.' Only when Grobler began to talk about Coode and his future, did Foster know that the seat was his.

Foster was in, alongside Cracknell, Pinsent and Redgrave. Coode was paired with Searle. The eight would contain Andrew Lindsay, Ben Hunt-Davis, Simon Dennis, Louis Attrill, Luka Grubor, Kieran West, Fred Scarlett and Steve Trapmore, coxed by Rowley Douglas.

'Ed and I had shared a room together in Australia for three weeks, we'd sat alongside each other on rowing machines, eaten together, rowed together, each of us wondering who made the boat go faster,' says Foster. 'We'd virtually been married to each other. Yet he was my biggest threat to a gold medal. I never wished him harm, and I am sure he would say the same about me.'

Coode and Foster shook.

'Well done,' said Coode, to whom the decision came as a relief. He was big about it, and accepted the decision graciously and magnanimously. As he later said, 'I knew where I was going.' By the time of the press conference, Coode had exited the scene. The five were four once more. Cracknell braced himself for Spandau Ballet; Foster fortified himself against 'the smell of James's lousy shoes'. But first: they had to row 20 kilometres.

'No drama,' smiled Grobler.

The music had finally stopped and the *placements* of the British Olympic rowing party were settled with everyone happy, except for a supremely miffed Bobby Thatcher, who, having failed to get a row at Atlanta when Cracknell, his double-scull partner, had been struck with tonsillitis, had just failed to make the coxless four when trialled back in early 1997, and was now being left out of the eight and therefore out of the Olympics.

The coxless four – pride of the fleet – contained one oarsman carrying an 8 kilogram tube of fat, another who was 37 years old with diabetes, colitis and a fractured arm, a third physically on the small side, rendered smaller still by the removal of two discs from his spine, and a fourth who was declared fit but prone to obsessive behaviour, tonsural instability and temperamental outbursts. This was Great Britain's safest bet for gold.

11

All For One and One For Four

May 2000

One May morning on the eve of the European regatta season, Cracknell stood up in the Leander gym and declared that he was having problems with Emily, his girlfriend, a Danish lightweight sculler and daughter of an Olympic gold-medallist oarsman (coxless four). The crew looked at him askance but were inclined to shrug and carry on pumping iron.

The crew knew that Cracknell drew the dividing line between rowing life and private life more heavily in favour of rowing than anyone else. Whereas the other three could switch off, Cracknell took rowing home. If the outing went badly, Emily suddenly couldn't cook. It was something Cracknell would just have to learn to get into balance. But this time, Emily was getting fed up. A student at Reading University, she decided to move out of Henley and live nearer college. Cracknell couldn't hack it. He'd lost 5 kilograms and a lot of sleep.

'You can call me a wanker if you like,' he persisted. 'Jürgen already has.'

For Cracknell to send up an emotional distress flare was not in itself unusual. Had Pinsent blurted out the same speech, that would have been grave indeed; but every grumble, complaint, whinge or gripe that Cracknell uttered had to have the Cracknell discount factored into it before being properly assessed.

'Breaking up with Em affected me really badly,' he wrote on the crew's website, 'as I blamed it [rowing] for mucking up my relationship and making me a pain to be with. I didn't really focus on training, went out with my mates and lost interest for a while so my form suffered.'

He had also broken two rules: first, control the controllable. Girlfriends were deemed controllable items, whereas a non-controllable might be, say, the weather, or the possibility of rival crews taking illegal performance-enhancing drugs. One's personal temperament, as befits an Olympic gold-medallist, was deemed eminently controllable, but Cracknell was at the mercy of his mercurial nature.

The second rule he'd broken was that what was off the water remained off the water. A central tenet of the brotherhood of the four was that the two lives – rowing and non-rowing – were kept apart by a strict but unwritten apartheid. Failure to achieve this suggested lack of requisite self-discipline to be an Olympic gold-medallist. Private lives were fodder only for light-hearted crew banter, not a source of anxiety about what extra-curricular activities your crew-mates got up to. Redgrave's diabetes, for example, was an off-the-water issue. It had potential on-the-water ramifications, but Redgrave handled it so that they never, or rarely, impinged when it mattered.

Not that the crew were unsympathetic towards Cracknell, they just thought he was exaggerating. 'James gave the impression that everything had gone downhill *dramatically*,' says Foster. 'To us, things seemed merely to have gone down-hill. James is not a tough guy in the traditional "I feel no pain, I'm tough because I shout about it" sense. You know James is pretty tough when it counts, but we knew we had to help, so we rallied round.'

....

'Would you like us to move in?' half-joked Redgrave.

Foster and Redgrave invited Cracknell for dinner. Pinsent took him to the cinema.

'Given how close we were and how intense things got between us,' says Foster, 'relationships were comparatively shallow. Matthew kept quiet about his new girlfriend until we'd found out about her from other sources. A lot of the fun of the four was that trust and relationship that we had. Had James desperately needed us, sure, we would have moved in.'

Cracknell and Emily eventually reunited in time for the Games.

The squad was more ironically than obviously macho: *Oh yes, 20 kilometres on the ergo here we come ... I'm really looking forward to this morning's maximum squat test*. None of them was the type who'd book singleton holidays at Club Yob, Ibiza. Redgrave and Pinsent thought Foster the most laddish of the crew, only because he partied hard, had a schizophrenic wardrobe and appeared with different girl-friends. Pinsent, although nine months younger than Foster, seemed considerably more grown-up and reserved. When he was 25, Pinsent was going on 52. Redgrave, meanwhile, was already practically a pipe-and-slippers man.

None of the four took themselves *too* seriously. Despite tension and hard times, crew-mates rarely fall out or fail to find common ground. Those rowers who aren't natural, affable, team players very soon learn the skills of group rela-tionships. In 2000 the four was off on training camps or at regattas for one day in every two. Some aspects of their relationships became very close. Others never got beyond that of the most basic friendship. They didn't need to. There was a 'guy thing' of mutual trust and understanding.

A sense of humour, however, was essential. Cracknell bore the brunt of everyone else's jokes, because he took them so well. Redgrave, who had never rowed with anyone as keen as

Cracknell, would tease him about being so serious. Even Grobler joined in. Cracknell might tell everyone where to go, but nothing was ever meant or taken badly. Foster took a joke, so long as it was about being laid-back or unpunctual. Redgrave suffered the endless 'old man' jokes in good heart. Everyone leapt at the chance to laugh at Pinsent, because he beat the squad at almost all the important physical tests that Grobler threw at them, but also because he was prone to seriousness. He always liked to sit in the front passenger seat of the crew minibus. One day, at camp in Varese in northern Italy in 2000, the squad minibus driver found a steering wheel from an old motor launch and attached it to a piece of wood, which he wedged inside the glove compartment, making it look like dual controls. How everyone laughed when Pinsent boarded the minibus to be flummoxed by this prop. Funniest of all was that Pinsent himself couldn't see the funny side of it.

The tedium or tension of the training programme was broken up with knocking-a-can-off-a-wall-type games. Every Sunday after training, the squad played five-a-side football in the field outside the Leander Club (the pitch turns into one of the car parks during Henley Royal Regatta), with jumpers for goals, thirty minutes each way, and Grobler refereeing. Redgrave played with gusto. If he was one goal down with five minutes to go, he'd up the intensity, sliding into two-footed tackles.

'He hates to be beaten in anything,' said Cracknell. 'Well, cards is OK. But five-a-side football matches are more like rugby, especially when he's losing.'

Foster recalls jumping over one particular challenge that would have put him off games for weeks. The safest place to stand was in goal. The ball would never go near you. Bethan Bell graciously agreed to play in goal for one of the squad's matches. Foster, who fantasised about scoring for Spurs in the FA Cup Final, 'seemed marginally better at football than the rest of the Great Britain rowing squad,' she said. 'This may have something to do with the fact that I was in goal for the opposition and while the other players were a little more gentlemanly, Tim had no qualms about firing the ball at me at 60 mph.'

Redgrave and Pinsent often unwound over golf. In fact, they more than unwound. They'd take it so seriously that there was a danger it might impact on their training. Cracknell fretted about stolen hours spent on the fairways. Grobler grew concerned too. On a couple of occasions, Matt and Steve left training feeling tired, played golf feeling more tired, and arrived the following morning for training feeling very tired.

Cracknell was upset. 'I think you should pay more attention to your training,' he told them.

The point was reached at which Redgrave and Pinsent felt they had to pull on their Pringles in hiding.

The day before the crew flew to Munich for the World Cup regatta in June 2000, Redgrave and Pinsent persuaded Cracknell and Foster to join them at golf. A points system was devised, complete with handicap. The pair that won the most points would have breakfast paid for by the losers the following morning at the airport. The pair that won the most holes would have their luggage carried and would be addressed as 'My Lord'.

The match teed off in a spirit of competitive fun. Cracknell proved particularly frustrating to Pinsent and Redgrave. With no semblance of finesse about his game – he was all forearms and muscle – he whacked the ball incredible distances. At the eighteenth tee, the pairs totted up their scores and found they were dead level. The final hole would be the decider. Pinsent drove the ball magnificently, but long. It fetched up in the rough. Redgrave and Foster played good-ish shots. Cracknell, a novice, was allowed an extra shot. Pinsent and Redgrave then cracked. Pinsent couldn't find his ball. Redgrave fluffed his second shot. Foster managed to chip his second to one side of the green, and found himself with 15 yards between his ball and the hole with three shots in hand to win. Foster practised the perfect swing, addressed the ball, swung and ... completely bottomed it. As luck would have it, he drilled the ball into a hump, which took the pace off it, and it came to rest six inches from the hole. Cracknell and Foster had won on both points and holes, albeit by a series of flukes.

The following day, a disgruntled Redgrave and Pinsent had to fork out, carry the bags and go through with the 'My Lord' routine. 'It was worth every minute,' says Foster. 'The breakfast was much better than any money. To have them call you "My Lord" before the entire British rowing squad, was deeply satisfying.' Redgrave and Pinsent hated it and demanded a rematch. Knowing that lightning would never strike twice in the same place, Cracknell and Foster adroitly wormed out of the challenge.

Many people remarked how Redgrave was cutting a mellower figure than of late. On cold, damp mornings, when training was not going to his liking, his brooding silences might still feel threatening and his commitment was still unshatterable, but he seemed to be enjoying himself far more than in the build-up to the Atlanta Games. Pre-Atlanta, Redgrave appeared to know everything about rowing except how to enjoy it. He had developed a large arsenal of professionally grim personae which he'd put on. They ranged from very, very bleakly grim indeed at the bottom of the scale, via disconsolately grim, all the way up to dour and resigned whenever he'd won an inconsequential race – so unlike the Redgrave that his crew-mates knew. As the four progressed, he seemed to be more confident about dropping the mask and replacing it with his cheerier private self.

Gone were the monosyllabic answers, the surly (which, as

a pun on 'Searle', has different connotations when used in a rowing context) expressions and intense glower that said, 'I'm the only professional in a sport of amateurs (you pygmies).' Now, at press conferences, Foster might whisper something and Redgrave would laugh and smile. Three years earlier he'd never have dreamt of smiling in public. The new 'old' Redgrave, the normal guy who enjoyed a laugh, began to emerge. Foster and Cracknell prided themselves on their influence.

'He still has the same ability to be focused, but my impression now is that he is having fun too,' said Foster. 'He's late for things now, because he knows I'll be even later. He's more of a laugh. Steve didn't realise what he got out of rowing. He'd done it for so long that it had become just another day in the office. We showed Steve that it was OK to laugh and enjoy yourself while still being "professional". Now he comes across so much better. I noticed it at our very first press conference. He seemed happy. At another press conference at Henley in 1998, Roxane Still [daughter of Athole Still, Redgrave's manager] remarked on how different Steve was compared with the Steve of two years earlier. She thought James and I brought out a fun side of him. We were generally more outgoing than Matthew had been when he paired with Steve. Matt and Steve admitted that James and I – keen and enthusiastic – gave them fresh impetus and a vitality transfusion.'

Foster and Cracknell had to think hard when asked if they'd seen Redgrave drunk. 'Whenever he is, so are we.'

Saturday, 17 June 2000

Cracknell had managed to secure three tickets to watch Germany play England in the European Championships. The match was an evening kick-off in Charleroi, in Belgium. How to get there after training that Saturday and return in time for the 8 a.m. start the following morning without Redgrave, Pinsent or Grobler finding out? Cracknell, Foster and Bobby Thatcher went into a huddle and hatched a plan.

After training at Dorney rowing lake near Windsor (where the crew were trying out Eton College's new rowing course), Cracknell said goodbye to Redgrave and Pinsent and leapt into Foster's car on the pretext of driving with him to Oxford. Instead of turning left outside Dorney, they hung a right and sped directly to Dover, where they picked up Bobby Thatcher (down-to-earth chap, amusing, stockily built, on the small side for an oarsman). The three oarsmen caught the ferry to Belgium and drove to Charleroi.

Cracknell had acquired the tickets via a friend at McDonald's. Their seats turned out to be located exactly one row behind and directly adjacent to Kevin Keegan, the England manager, and the England substitutes' bench. This was a massive cockroach in the ointment. Any shot of Keegan would inevitably show the three oarsmen sitting behind him. Redgrave, something of a football fan (Chelsea), would no doubt be watching.

Panicked, Foster, Cracknell and Thatcher debated how they'd explain away or excuse any sightings. They stayed firmly glued to their seats, desperate to keep a low profile, throughout the game, especially when Alan Shearer scored the only goal and the English fans erupted. After the game, the trio jumped into Foster's car and raced back to the Channel, only to miss the last ferry home. They had an hour's 'rest' in Foster's car before catching the next ferry at 4.30 a.m.

They arrived back in Henley at 6.30 a.m., ready for training at 7.30 a.m. They managed to complete the day's work without any visible signs of distress or without any of the rest of the squad finding out, although there was a nasty moment when Redgrave was closely studying a match report in the sports section of one of the Sunday papers, which showed a picture of Keegan and behind him … the man who had been sitting next to Foster; but Foster himself had been mercifully cropped out. After training, Foster bumped into Bob, the Leander cleaner.

'See the game on television last night?' Bob asked.

'Not on television,' replied Foster, slipping Bob a match programme. There was a confused silence followed by a colourful tirade in which Bob implied that he knew Foster's parents and that Foster should get to know himself a lot better as soon as possible.

'We survived training,' said Foster, 'got home and slept for the rest of the day. It was worth it. It was the only game England won in the championships.'

12

Build-up to Sydney

That summer, something of the sparkle and authority of the crew seemed to be missing, with somewhat critical timing, as this was the last regatta season before the Olympics. At Munich regatta, France chased the British four and only lost to them by a diminishing 0.76 seconds. Redgrave afterwards brushed aside concerns with, 'It's too early in the season to pull too far ahead. We know we have more in hand but we don't want to use it until we have to.'

'It's all part of the plan to win with the minimum of effort,' echoed Pinsent; but the bravado was looking increasingly forced.

Three weeks later at Vienna international regatta, the four only just beat New Zealand, Italy and Australia in a race that was far harder than anticipated. They had thought they had another gear, but only realised they didn't when they looked for it.

1–2 July 2000

At Henley Royal Regatta, the four confronted the Australian national four – not the Oarsome Foursome, who had by this time disbanded, but the Sydney-based crew of James Stewart, Ben Dodwell, Geoff Stewart and Bo Hanson, runners-up to the British four at the 1999 World Championships in St Catherine's. As the race started beneath leaden skies, rain showered down and a headwind whipped up. God was weeping at the crew's final appearance at Henley.

Steering erratically, Leander led by a canvas at the Barrier and by half a length at Fawley. From then on, the Australians never dropped their rate below 40, while Leander struck 38. At the Mile, the Australians had reduced Leander's lead to two feet. As the crews passed the enclosures, a gruff voice sang out, 'Come on, Aussie, come on, come on,' answered by a clipped voice calling, 'Come on, Leander!' That got the crowd going. Leander wound the rate up to 43 and were cheered home by two thirds of a length.

7–9 July 2000

Six days later, at Lucerne international Regatta, their final competition before the Olympics, the crew found themselves mired in a three-day monsoon. God was still crying. In the semi-final, the four led for the first 1500 metres, then curiously fell apart when they upped the rate. New Zealand beat them by one tenth of a second, the first loss for the Pinsent-Foster-Redgrave-Cracknell combination. They attributed the result to their stupidity and misjudgement. Worse was to come.

As the crew warmed up for their final, a squall added to the downpour. When it rains at Lucerne, the temperature drops very rapidly. Foster had never felt so cold before a race as on that day and was shivering at the Start despite thirty minutes' warming up. Wearing T-shirts designed to keep them cool in hot weather, the crew shivered on the Start. The Italians took an early lead and continued at what the British four reckoned was an unsustainable pace. When Britain settled, New Zealand carved straight through them. Foster looked around for what the Italians were doing, but they'd blown Britain out of the water. With 750 metres to go, Britain was still level with Australia, but finding it a slog. Then the Australians blasted through too and even overtook New Zealand. Italy won, Australia came second, New Zealand third and Great Britain fourth. It was a conclusive thrashing. In the space of less than one week, the riggers, oars and everything else had fallen off the British boat, reducing the crew from world-beaters to mediocrities. Now four crews – the Italians, New Zealanders, Australians and British – would go to Sydney believing they could win.

'That final felt really strange,' says Foster. 'The boat felt underpowered. My impression was that Steve struggled to put together two races in two days. He had taped sugar to the inside of the boat, and just before the race made a point of checking his blood sugar, which was unusual.'

Planted and wrapped in Foster's disappointment was a foreboding that their fall from grace might prompt ruinous change. The inevitable media chorus of 'Redgrave over the hill!' was readily distracted only by Tim Henman and the British tennis team losing to Ecuador in the Davis Cup. The worshipful media desperately wanted a happy ending to the Redgrave story. A deafening silence emanated from Wapping and Canary Wharf, punctuated only by the sound of obituarists politely sharpening their pencils.

Grobler seemed to take it worse than Redgrave himself. 'It's terrible,' he fumed, 'after what you've done for British sport and British rowing, now they're having a go at you.'

In fact, any mention of Redgrave's age and any doubts cast on the likelihood of his fifth Olympic gold medal did nothing but spur the crew while unleashing the inordinate strength of a Redgrave possessed, not something any in-the-know rival would have wished for. But first, the crew took a rare, albeit scheduled, mid-season break. Cracknell went to Copenhagen to salvage his relationship.

Monday, 17 July 2000

They were the fittest, strongest and most technically gifted crew, but they'd lost. What was plan B? One week after Lucerne, the crew met at Leander to ask what, indeed, plan B was.

Grobler stood up and took responsibility for Lucerne. 'I asked you to race at Henley, which was tough, because we had to race the Australians. We trained hard between Henley and Lucerne. Then I asked you to race in Lucerne ...' The crew nodded acceptance.

More positively, they acknowledged that Lucerne wasn't so much a learning curve as a ski-jump from which they'd ended up off piste. Their reliance on power had made them overlook their flaws. Standards had slipped, technical niggles were obtruding. Once more, Foster delicately raised the matter of the crew's weight. At 113 kilograms Pinsent was still 8 kilograms over. Redgrave weighed 108 kilograms, against his usual 105. At 88 kilograms, Foster himself weighed 2 kilograms too many.

'I'm not saying that was why we lost,' he said, 'but if statistics are to be believed, 15 kilograms of excess weight would make the difference. None of us would want to race in a boat that was 15 kilos overweight, now would we?'

The point seemed to stick. No one turned around and screamed, 'Tim, you weren't pulling hard enough.'

The meeting proved constructive. Cracknell wasn't suicidal or reduced to a state of diminished responsibility or convinced that everything had gone wrong and that the crew needed to train three times as hard and radically change its approach. Redgrave wasn't aggressive towards himself or anyone else. It was a decisive moment.

'Had we won at Lucerne, we would definitely have lost the Olympics,' says Foster. 'It gave us the kick we needed. We realised things had been sliding.'

It seemed to work. As Pinsent cut back on the death platters and trained harder, the kilograms tumbled off him. From that meeting up until the Olympic final, you could not have met five more dedicated professional people pulling their weight for the crew, whether it was Jürgen tweaking and analysing the programme and controlling the logistics, or the crew addressing technical weaknesses, physical flaws and mental distractions. Much work was needed; much work was done. There was a noticeable tightening of the crew bond. 'We had something to work against now which maybe we hadn't had before Lucerne,' says Foster. 'We knew there were other crews who wanted to win that gold medal. It wasn't ours by right.'

Another reason for the disastrous showing at Lucerne was the boat itself. After Henley Royal Regatta, Cracknell complained that his position at bow felt uncomfortable. For Cracknell to complain about anything was regarded as background noise, despite his new-found authority. When Grobler tried swapping Cracknell with Pinsent, Matthew immediately complained about the bow seat too, while Cracknell thought the stroke position felt fantastic. Everyone sat up and took notice. The crew needed a new boat.

A coxless four measures 13 metres long by 55 centimetres at its widest. It consists of a carbon fibre shell wrapped around a carbon fibre rib structure, designed with the sole aim of translating the movements of the crew into boat speed using the leverage afforded by a combination of oars and sliding seats. You don't so much sit in a boat as balance on top of it. Its overriding specifications are lightness and stiffness. The British coxless four (with riggers and seats) weighed 50.2 kilograms (the minimum permitted weight was 50 kilograms;

the crew itself officially weighed 388 kilograms). During the crew's three and a half years together, they worked their way through eight boats, as successive marques rapidly became obsolete or lost their stiffness due to the forces the crew exerted on them.

The history of racing boats is about weight reduction and hull stiffness. In the early nineteenth century, crews rowed in clinker-built tubs with fixed seats. The River and Rowing Museum in Henley-on-Thames displays the boat in which Oxford University rowed the first Oxford vs Cambridge Boat Race in 1829. It looks more like something you'd harpoon a whale in. In those days, the rowing stroke involved heaving at the oar using only your upper body, arms and shoulders, as in a hired rowing boat on a municipal lake. The advent of outriggers allowed a slimmed-down hull. Sliding seats, invented in 1870, allowed the oarsman to apply his leg muscles to the stroke. Boat builders developed delicate shells by steaming wafer-thin sheets around a wooden structure, which produced a light, stiff craft. The advent of carbon fibre in the 1970s opened up a new dimension of lightness and stiffness. Nowadays, all top-level crews use carbon fibre shells and oars.

While shells have become lighter and stiffer, oarsmen are growing bigger and heavier. The average weight of the Cambridge eight that rowed in the first Boat Race was 11 stones 1¾ pounds (70.6 kilograms). The average weight of Redgrave, Cracknell, Foster and Pinsent was 100.7 kilograms. We are heading towards the boatless boat, the oarless oar, the leviathan crew and the high-tech boat.

The new shell was a top-of-the-range – nay bespoke – craft, which proved the most expensive racing shell of all time. The initial cost was £6000. Aylings of Weybridge in Surrey had built the boat to the crew's instructions. The specification was to shoehorn 400 kilograms of muscle, ego and ambition into the smallest frame possible. Internal dimensions were tailored to the crew. Fitting Pinsent's 6 foot 6 inch frame and size 14 feet into the tapering stern of the boat proved particularly tricky. The strong, light hull was streamlined against expected crosswinds, for which Penrith was famous. Air was funnelled between the oarsmen. The foredeck was contoured to meet the bowman's back. The steering mechanism was concealed below deck. Grobler wanted 139 centimetres between each seat, as opposed to the standard 142. The shortened weight-distribution would reduce the boat's see-sawing as the crew moved up and down their slides. The deep, narrow hull was based on an East German profile. She was a very hot ship indeed, the Excalibur of shells, affording great acceleration, but twitchiness at low-pressure paddling.

It was delivered shortly before the British fleet was due to depart for Australia. At the last minute, Grobler decided to check its weight. Cracknell stood on a set of scales and hefted the boat himself. It appeared to be a few kilograms overweight. Another set of scales was found and the boat was perched atop the two sets. It was definitely overweight, by 3 kilograms, equivalent to 0.75 seconds over 2000 metres. Aylings had made a mistake. They had just enough time to make a new one.

The problem had arisen because Grobler had originally wanted to use lightweight carbon fibre riggers. Tested at Dorney rowing lake near Windsor earlier that summer, the riggers had wobbled as if improperly fastened to the side of the boat. Tightening the nuts didn't help, so the crew reverted to heavier conventional aluminium riggers. Aylings hadn't allowed for this. Grobler did the talking.

Adrian Morris, an enthusiastic ex-oarsman and Aylings' boss, agreed to pay for a new boat and shipping to Australia. Total cost: £29,982.

The exact specifications of the coxless four are:

Length: 12.85 metres
Weight: 50.3 kilograms
Weight of crew: 430 kilograms
Outriggers: Len Neville, Staines
Oars: Dreissigacker, Vermont, USA.

While Aylings got to work, the crew packed off their 1988 boat. When the new lighter shell was delivered to the Leander Club, the crew managed a quick outing before flying.

Foster flew out to Australia one day ahead of his crew-mates to give his back a chance to recover from the flight. Arriving at Heathrow comfortably (read: scruffily) dressed, Foster couldn't work out what was going on when the check-in desk tore up his ticket and he was suddenly being greeted by a superior air hostess and personally escorted on to the plane. It turned out that his seat had been upgraded by Larry Tracey, an entrepreneur friend of Mike Spracklen, who did his bit for the British rowing team by upgrading the crew from Business Class to First Class.

'I was seated so far to the front of the aeroplane, I thought they were going to ask me to fly it,' says Foster. 'The stopover in Singapore was an inconvenience, whereas in cattle class it would have been a relief.' Foster manfully resisted the fine wines on offer.

Two days after the squad had settled into their training camp in Queensland, a long wooden crate arrived containing their new boat in one piece.

At the Queensland training camp, not a single detail had escaped the eye of the British Olympic Association. Athletes from other sports were present too. 'It was a fantastic camp,' says Foster, 'and a real precursor to the Olympic Village. You felt part of a big picture, part of an Olympic team.'

At Hinze Dam a 2000 metre course was buoyed out in the main bowl of the lake, from which several fingers radiated outwards. These fingers could be used for long outings of up to 16 kilometres with just one turnaround. Rolling green hills planted with vineyards fringed the lake. Eagles soared overhead. Besides the sound of the crew rowing, the scene was utterly silent and had a sense of being untouched by human hands. It was the perfect pre-Olympic camp.

The four worked on its technical weaknesses, concentrating on applying more power at the front end of the stroke. As they trained alongside the men's eight, coxless pair and women's crews, the all-important 'sum is greater than the parts' togetherness began to emerge, and their speed picked up. The blades gripped the water as if it were a solid thing. The syncopation, rhythm, balance, power, length of stroke, speed at the catch, the spring of the leg-and-shoulder drive, the power, the deftness at the finish as the blades flashed out of the water in unison, the rattle of the oars in their gates at the feather, and then that glorious – aaaaaaaaaaaargh – run on the boat. You could also hear bubbles beneath the boat as it cut through the meniscus, signalling flight through the plane. All the ingredients and motions were there in machine-like uniformity. Herein lay the inexplicable bliss of rowing, a curious thrill, hard to express in words, but one that will ever remain the delight of an esoteric few and ought really to be classified as a Class A drug. It was so much more than mere compensation for the hardships of the journey behind them, the bleak midwinter outings in snow and rain, the buffeting of wind and waves, the discomforts of rough water and an uneven boat, never mind the illnesses and injuries picked up on the way. One could row like this for ever.

'We left Hinze Dam having achieved three weeks' work in eighteen days,' says Foster. 'The crew was more clear-sighted. There was a renewed focus on ideas. To an external eye we hadn't changed much, but we all addressed what we thought was the way forwards. If Jürgen wanted to increase the training, there were immediate nods of acceptance. If James made a comment from the bow seat, all it would require would be one call from him to get four uniform reactions, rather than four calls and one reaction. During all our training pieces, we measured the speed of the boat using a Pacecoach device. Speeds that had previously been top end became the norm. There was a renewed sense of purpose. Having spent four years thinking the gold medal was in our grasp, we'd let it slip. Now we were reclaiming our destiny.'

Just before the squad left for Sydney, Pinsent was asked to say a few words about preparations for the Olympic Village. He addressed the men's and women's rowing teams, and chatted things through. He spoke about what to expect in the Village, how you'd feel when you arrived, the excitement of it all, and how unnerving it could be. His message was: be prepared; don't do anything stupid.

The crew were handed out their kit. The full British Olympic Association official kit amounted to a considerable inventory of clothing: a dozen T-shirts, half a dozen long-sleeved tops, tracksuit, trainers and the marching uniform for the opening ceremony – which filled two suitcases that you get given too. You were obliged to wear these clothes throughout the Games.

The four were used to kit protocols. Training or competing, they had to display their sponsor's logo. If spotted 'wrongly' dressed, even scattering ducks and swans on a dawn training outing at Henley, a well-starched suit might have a quiet word with them afterwards. At Atlanta, Redgrave, who was then sponsored by Adidas, had been caught out. Popping over to the laundrette, he'd thrown on a Russell Athletic T-shirt. On the way, he had bumped into Mr Adidas. A deeply embarrassed Redgrave was thereafter a stickler for correct kit.

Grobler never wore kit at regattas. His 'smart-casual' jeans and polo shirt were a well-rehearsed front. Among East European rowing coaches, there was an unwritten sartorial code, which Grobler heeded to the unwritten letter: in training, one flaunted the full official Great Britain kit for the benefit of whatever ducks, swans and suits were present during early-morning outings; at international regattas, before the gaze of the rowing world, one did smart-casual – jeans and a short-sleeved shirt – to impress upon other coaches and oarsmen that one's crews were so exquisitely tuned that no further coaching was possible. The other East European coaches followed suit. All those coaches who, like Grobler, had migrated west after the Soviet empire crumbled, could be found on the morning of international regattas in a huddle, uniformly dressed down, having a laugh: 'Ho-ho, my crew is ready' ... 'Ha-ha, mine is more ready than yours.' In contrast, many dilatory Western coaches spent the days before a big race cycling furiously alongside their charges, emblazoned in full coaching regalia accessorised with stopwatches and rating watches, barking into megaphones. Grobler never even packed a bicycle.

'Why not?' Foster once asked.

Grobler shrugged. 'Because we're ready.'

13

Village Idiots

The four arrived at Sydney in high spirits, keen to show the world they had rebounded. Pinsent was down to a svelte 105 kilograms. Redgrave had lost between 3 and 4 kilograms, and Foster had shed a couple of kilograms.

Built on an old munitions dump, the Olympic Village squeezed athletes into apartments destined to be sold as flats. Warned to expect matchboxes, the British rowing team found marginally more spacious shoeboxes and sardine tins. The rowing eight (nine, if you include the cox), the coxless pair of Greg Searle and Ed Coode, Matt Wells (the single sculler), and the coxless four were squeezed into a 'four-bedroom flat' partitioned into eight bedrooms barely large enough for two single beds each. Foster shared with Cracknell. Visible from their window, the Olympic flame, lit during the opening ceremony, seemed to symbolise their hopes for the days ahead.

For three weeks this was the squad's home. The token furniture, tiny kitchen and lack of privacy hardly mattered. Meals were taken in the Olympic food tent and, since Penrith was a forty-five-minute drive away, most of the day seemed to be spent either at the rowing lake, or travelling to and fro.

Star athletes don't do the Village. At Barcelona, the US

basketball team checked into a hotel over 300 miles away in Monaco; professional tennis players wouldn't be seen dead in the Village. At Sydney, Redgrave was the big draw, but he never demanded special treatment, or any treatment at all – so long as the transport worked, people didn't nag him about winning gold, and no one near him went down with a contagious illness. No minders, aides or garish-suited handlers barred access or issued sound bites. The king of the water enjoyed no regal or palatial trappings about his mode of transport or billet when representing his country. He room-shared with Pinsent and travelled by bus.

Although the Olympic Village housed thousands of athletes, it could be a curiously lonely place. Garbed in the official kit, one's compatriots were instantly recognisable. Yet a friendly figure in the distance so often might not, on closer inspection, reveal a friendly face. You might queue up in the food tent with your teammates, then lose them in the teeming track-suited throng as you fetched a bread roll. To avoid losing touch with each other, the four staked out its own table, and welcomed in stray squad members. This may sound silly and 'junior school', but when you're under pressure, it is a comfort to break bread with friends.

Among the many potential hazards and temptations lying in wait in the strange and exciting land of the Olympic Village, the food tent is the biggest temptation of the lot. More gold medals have been won and lost in Olympic food tents than you'd credit. The Sydney food tent seated 4000 and was open twenty-four hours a day, seven days a week, free of charge. It offered at least twenty national cuisines and their equivalent fast foods. No dietary regime or intolerance or religious observance was too far-flung not to be catered for. It was undeniably impressive even to athletes from the well-fed West. To athletes from hungrier parts it was almost irresistible. Some felt like Dickensian urchins gone to heaven. Eastern bloc competitors would see free McDonald's and go berserk. You could pick up a plate or bowl – or two plates or bowls – pile them high and stuff yourself like a Strasbourg goose. Cases of athletes coming off training regimes and putting on half a stone during the Games as a result of food-tent binges were not uncommon. Fortunately for the oarsmen, they could temporarily shun this cornucopia. The week-long Olympic regatta traditionally ends with the Games only half done, leaving the whole of the second week free for gorging with total impunity.

Pity the poor athletes whose events took place towards the end of the Olympic fortnight. In week two, psyched-up athletes still competing in the Games would rise early and nibble rabbit food or eat raw eggs in preparation for their event later in the day, while other athletes, their competition over, would be staggering back to the food tent for a pre-bedtime binge having partied all night. After the Olympic regatta at Atlanta, Foster and Cracknell returned from a party at 6 a.m. and dived into the McDonald's section of the food tent (where, earlier on, Richard Wearne, the Australian oarsman, had stuffed away five Big Macs in one sitting). A well-refreshed Cracknell found himself striking up conversation with Max Sciandri, the British cyclist, stiffly breakfasting in preparation for his event.

'So, are you looking forward to tomorrow, Max?'

'Er, my race is today, and, yes, I'm looking forward to it.'

'. . . So, Max,' persisted Cracknell, glazed-eyed. 'How, how do you think you're gonna do . . . tomorrow?'

'Er, as I've said, my race is today.'

It took five minutes for Cracknell's brain to twig what Sciandri was saying. He felt profoundly embarrassed. Sciandri won bronze in the road race.

In the second week of the Olympics, you tried to avoid athletes still in competition. Jonathan Edwards, the triplejumper, took a pre-Sydney swipe at the swimming team, saying how difficult he found Village life, because, after the first morning of competition, when so many swimmers had been knocked out, the Games turned into a two-week party (although, to be fair, the British swimming team at Sydney made a pact that none of them would touch alcohol until the last of them had dived in for his or her final race). The swimmers exacted sweet revenge at the World Championships of 2002 when some of the women competitors said how hard it had been to concentrate because Jonathan Edwards had been out partying so hard.

A classic, and in retrospect hilarious, example of serial food abuse occurred at the Barcelona Olympics. Two days before the Games opened, the entire Great Britain women's rowing team was struck down with upset stomachs. It was terribly bad luck, or good luck, depending on your loyalties. Curiously, none of the oars*men* had suffered, despite living in the same building as the women and eating the same food. The problem was traced back to an ice-cream stall that stood between the rowing course and the rowers' accommodation block. Walls, the ice cream makers, had just introduced the Magnum, a choc ice on a stick that was irresistible to British oarswomen. This stall was dishing them out gratis. It was calculated that each oarswoman in the Great Britain Olympic team was devouring on average six Magnums a day, enough to make anyone feel sick.

Food isn't the only potential Olympic hazard. Just before the Barcelona Olympics, Brian Miller, an Australian psychologist, had been contracted by the British Olympic Association to work with the British rowing team. He had briefed the oarsmen on pitfalls that awaited the unsuspecting athlete with unaccustomed time and energy on his hands.

'You'd be surprised at the stupid things athletes do,' he said. 'They're feeling tense and they're only training one hour each day instead of six.' One cautionary tale involved an Australian middle-distance runner who panicked when he saw one of his rivals lifting weights in a gym placed at athletes' disposal. 'Mmmm,' he thought, 'that guy's in my event, and he's lifting weights. But I've never been to a gym before, never mind lifted weights.' Following this line of paranoia, he went into the gym and accidentally put his back out.

Miller's wisdom came diced in quotable McNuggets.

'If you row a good race, there are people who will come up to you and tell you you're fantastic,' he told the squad. 'But you must have your bullshit filters switched on or they'll piss in your pockets. Don't lose sight of what you've done and have to do.'

Not even the bedrooms could be trusted. Cracknell room-shared with Foster. Their beds were stackable bunk beds. To save space, they fixed one bed on top of the other. One night, Cracknell leapt down from his top bunk, switched off the light, then clambered back up. There followed what sounded like a loud explosion, except that it wasn't an explosion. It was the tremendous *ccccrrrraaaaackkk* of Cracknell and his bedside table collapsing in a heap on the floor.

'James? Are you OK?' asked Foster, after the noise had subsided.

'Ha-ha-ha-ha-ha-ha. Oh no! Ha-ha-ha-ha! We'll . . . ha-ha-ha . . . we'll wake Steve and Matthew . . . ha-ha . . . next door.'

Right on cue, the door burst open, the light snapped on and there stood Redgrave and Pinsent framed in the doorway, staring at Cracknell sprawled on the floor giggling his head off. Cracknell was fine. His bedside table lay flat-packed on the floor. Worse, his treasured collection of Oakley sunglasses, which he'd kept on the top shelf, lay shattered beneath the debris. The pre-Games safety briefing had said nothing about the dangers of low-budget Olympic furniture.

Cracknell carried with him umpteen pairs of sensational dark glasses. Dark glasses shield the eyes from the water's reflective glare, and are deemed technical items not subject to sponsor's decree. Anything goes, and, in Cracknell's case, anything went. For Sydney 2000, Oakley brought out a set of radical over-the-top glasses which discarded traditional earstems for a hingeless frame that wrapped and gripped the upper cranium. To Cracknell, they looked terrific. Redgrave thought otherwise. These ridiculous military night-vision goggles might spur the opposition. Semi-jokingly, but with undertones darker than anything in Cracknell's goggle collection, Redgrave suggested that, were he to wear those particular glasses, then he, Redgrave, might refuse to row with him. Later, during the track-and-field competition, Ato Bolden, the sprinter, was caught on camera wearing over-the-tops. The stadium erupted with laughter.

Besides that one furniture experience, the four treated Village facilities with kid-gloved respect.

14

Water's Edge

Tuesday, 19 September 2000

The crew was prepared for a stormy ride. Penrith, 40 kilometres west of Sydney, was reputedly a treacherous course. A certain weed, introduced to aerate the water, had grown wildly out of control. Clumps would die, float to the surface, foul rudders and fins, and generally mar regattas. The Internet grapevine had been thrashing about like an arcing live wire with tales of crews becoming entangled and disappearing.

Wind was another problem. Ever since the rowing world had packed up after Atlanta, it had been fretting about Penrith's crosswinds, white horses and rumours of regattas being blown away. Inevitably, the Sydney Games coincided with the most tempestuous season. Scaremongers predicted a fiasco. A whirlwind of rumour and counter-rumour began building up in chat rooms, blowing up a ferocious cyberstorm.

By the time the Games had opened, a rumoured six-figure sum had been spent draining the water, killing off the triffid, removing it, then refilling the lake. The wind was another matter. FISA's 'fairness committee' had drawn up plans for a processional time trial instead of the usual six-abreast first-past-the-post cavalry charge. If the weather cut up rough, the crews would start at thirty-second intervals and chase each other down the course. The scaremongers shrieked, 'Told you so!' when the Italian coxless four nearly sank a few days before the start of the regatta, forcing them to work out on rowing machines in their hotel car park. 'It's a joke,' said Carlo Monati of the Italian boat and a great hero in his native country. 'Rowing is for flat water, like swimming. It's not like sailing.' What if the course became unrowable? Would the medals be sorted out over a game of Battleships?

The shell of the British coxless four had been designed with a low above-the-water profile, cut-away bow and stern sections and wing-shaped aluminium riggers to cope with wind and waves. The Heath Robinson-esque steering mechanism and wires that connected one of Redgrave's shoes to the credit-card-sized rudder were hidden below deck.

So naturally, as if blessed, the four arrived at Penrith, to be greeted by a mastering azure smoothly reflected in a giant mirror, and flags limply hanging in the windless air. The weather stayed like that for the entire regatta.

Penrith is otherwise a fine rowing venue. A small warm-up lake runs parallel to the 2000 metre rowing course. Excellent facilities included a communal area with a large tent, vast television screens, and a smaller tent for each team.

The crew were annoyed at finding themselves seeded fourth. This meant that, instead of rowing against the hapless Poles, the British faced the fancied Australians in their heat. There was surprising tension within the crew, who reacted to type: Cracknell became nervous, Redgrave tetchy, Pinsent quiet and Foster chatty. They wanted to go off with a bang and prove that they had rebounded.

Their heat went exactly to plan. The crew dominated the race from the first stroke. At one point they were two lengths up on the field and cruised home comfortably ('We had an extra gear!'). It was convincing and authoritative. The Australians were definitely second best and trailing in Britain's wake, in a reversal of Lucerne. Anyone in that Australian crew would have known then and there that his dreams of Olympic glory were more or less dead.

'We have been favourites for most of the things we have done,' said Redgrave. 'The bottom line is that we know, if we row our best, no one can beat us ... history has proven that in those high-pressure situations, we have performed better than at any other time in our lives.'

Thursday, 21 September 2000

The four pushed off from the landing stage at Penrith shortly after dawn to warm up before their semi-final later that morning. They'd gone off in pairs. Bow pair – James Cracknell and Steve Redgrave – paddled, while stern pair – Tim Foster and Matthew Pinsent – sat at the 'easy all' position, blades skimming the water. As the blades broke the meniscus and levered the boat forward, the early morning stillness was broken by the crisp chopping of the blades into the water.

Then Pinsent leant over the side of the boat and made a noise like *hoiuuuuwwwwwwghghghbbbbbbllllleeeerrrrr*. 'Oh dear,' he said. 'I'm off again.'

'Good,' thought Tim Foster, smiling, as he watched Pinsent's regurgitated breakfast recede into the distance, a prettily coloured slick on the gently agitated surface of Penrith rowing lake. 'That means Matthew is as nervous as the rest of us.'

Pinsent hadn't appeared nervous, although you could never really tell. His innermost thoughts tightly buttoned up, Matthew wore his heart on the inside of his breast pocket, and normally projected an air of self-confidence and calmness, not his breakfast. Certain symptoms, however, betrayed his pre-race anxiety. Among these was a tendency for his last few helpings of food to go into reverse. His crew-mates seized this rare chance to laugh at his expense with delight. Redgrave grinned. No one saw Pinsent eat another mouthful for three days.

'That's better. Where were we?' said Pinsent.

'Back stops,' called Cracknell from up in the bows. 'Paddling light. Are you ready? Go!'

Tcha-aaaaaaaaargh ... tcha-aaaaaaaaargh ... tcha-aaaaaaaaargh ... tcha-aaaaaaaaargh ...

Within a few strokes, Foster's laughter was abruptly silenced. An alarming pang shot up his spine. 'Oh sh**!' he thought, as the cold hand of fear gripped his heart. The last thing he wanted on the morning of the Olympic semi-final was another back drama. He knew that the first five minutes of the outing would either soothe or inflame his back. The boat sliced through the Penrith mirror, Pinsent, Cracknell and Redgrave oblivious to Foster's state of near-panic as his former dread started up and writhed before his eyes.

As the paddling continued, Foster's back quietened down.

In their semi-final, the four never came under pressure, and won comfortably. Afterwards, Foster slunk off to find Mark Edgar, the rowing team's chief physiotherapist. He vainly tried to convince himself that his wanting to see Edgar was merely a cry for 'tender loving care', not an actual problem. After all, isn't it an iron rule among top athletes that whenever a physiotherapist is present, they will find compelling reasons to book appointments? Physiotherapists are one of the main causes of aching limbs and sore muscles among world-class athletes, aren't they?

During the 1994 World Rowing Championship at Indianapolis, the rowing team physios had been so overworked they'd had to stagger appointment times. Foster's back had risen to the big occasion by playing its usual trick of going *ping!* just before a heat. When he'd called on the physios, they'd been all booked up. 'Take my slot,' Greg Searle, Foster's crew-mate in the coxless four, had chirped. 'I'm not sure what's wrong with me yet.'

Really, it was the egos that needed massaging. Given the choice, who wouldn't want a comfort rub? Well, Foster wouldn't. His policy towards physical ailments was stoically to disregard them until they'd deteriorated to a point at which it was no longer feasible to do so. So for Foster actually to fess up to Edgar was only marginally less serious than fessing up to his crew-mates.

He felt blinding pain when bending over, and was adopting an awkward seated posture. If '1' was normal and '5' was 'unable to walk', this rated '3' on the Foster scale of dorsal episodes.

'Most of the pain was on the right-hand side,' he says, 'so I'd tend to compensate by shifting my weight to the left. These symptoms had become commonplace over the years. Honestly, my back has more sense than me.'

The bumpy forty-five minute bus ride between the Olympic Village and Penrith was to blame. Despite the best efforts of Foster's bespoke inflatable travel pillow, which contoured his back, the bus ride felt like osteoporosis on wheels.

If part of the role of physiotherapist is comforter and hand-holder, Edgar was far from typical of his profession. A 'very pragmatic' New Zealander whose Kiwi bluntness was unwhetted by thirteen years' living in England, he was never knowingly overgenerous with the TLC; not for Edgar touchy-feely herbal tea physiotherapy. As he manipulated and kneaded Foster's vertebrae and back muscles, Foster dreaded hearing, 'Strewth, myte, it's fufty-fufty. Do you want to take the chinz?'

'Mark is honest,' he thought. 'He knows I'll be honest with him. We've worked well together over the previous seven months. He knows I'm not the sort to cry wolf. I don't need TLC.'

'If we do what needs doing, it'll be foine,' said Edgar.

At the Olympic Village, Edgar set up a physiotherapy couch in the crew's sitting room. Foster had three sessions of physiotherapy that day, and three the following day. Physiotherapy was Foster's comfort blanket, Edgar his talisman. Even if Foster couldn't quite tick the box marked 'spine/back', he felt he could devolve the worrying on to Edgar.

That evening, Foster and Cracknell conducted their usual microscopically detailed post-mortem on the semi-final. Cracknell always liked to analyse the minutiae of the crew's daily performances, and Foster didn't mind indulging him, but kept quiet about his back. One thing was certain: no way was he going to broadcast this present flare-up. Some matters were for crew debate, others for private consumption only. Foster reckoned his back was firmly in the private camp. Top of the agenda was Matthew Pinsent chucking his breakfast.

'A nervous Pinsent is a Pinsent who is up for a big race,' explained Foster. 'For all but a few days every four years, Matthew exudes calm confidence. In the last few days before an Olympic Games, he *tries* to exude calm confidence. He believes he will win, but knows it will hurt. You want him nervous. Then he will come out fighting.'

Friday, 22 September

The eve of the final was a 'rest' day. The crew spent the morning at Penrith paddling the paddle of the gods. After the outing, they lifted the boat clear of the water and placed it on trestles, where Grobler wiped it down. They then left it on racks in the boat park among the five other coxless fours in the final. Back at the Village, they lunched, rested on the grass square outside Grobler's apartment, before heading in for the big pre-race.

15

The Man with the Hammer

23 September 2000

The crowds began to gather for the final soon after seven o'clock in the morning. The media descended en masse. The BBC presented that day's coverage of the Games lakeside from Penrith; every BBC hand not required elsewhere turned up. Every journalist not directly involved with another sport was there – the feature writers, colourists, 'parachutists' and 'picnickers', most of whom had already written their race reports, covering every eventuality. Chris Dodd, of the *Independent*, turned up just in time to watch the four complete their warm-up paddle.

'When they emerged from the mist and the crowd cheered, I just thought *God is in his heaven*,' he says. 'We were all on edge all week waiting for this damn final. There was a lot of speculation and nervousness in the air. So many people really wanted them to win – for Redgrave. A Kiwi chap told me he really wanted Redgrave to win, even though his son was in the New Zealand four.'

'Everyone knew the four had lost in Lucerne, so there was a feeling that everything was still up in the air,' says Dan Topolski, who commentated on the race for BBC Television. 'The crews who'd beaten them at Lucerne were all there in the final. You had this sense of an unbeaten record being severely dented at Lucerne, and you knew it would be a great race. So many hopes were riding on it.'

10.30 a.m.

By the time the race was due, some 35,000 people had gathered in brilliant morning sunshine. Two kilometres away, the six crews were fixed in place ready to go. The starter finished the roll-call; for a fraction of a second there was a moment of immense calm on board, as nerves suddenly fell silent.

EEEERRROOOOGH!

The 'process' took over: *first stroke, finish it off; second stroke, pick up the boat before it slows down; third stroke, use two-thirds of the slide* . . . The crew had been through the start so many times that it almost felt good to slip into a familiar routine.

'In the first minute, everything was frantic,' says Foster. 'The boat felt quite good. We always started fast. Whether we were up on the first stroke or not, I tried not to look. We were focused on our own rowing and on the boat, but we were locked on to putting in those first 15 strokes. Steve called for "rhythm" and the rate came down. It was about concentrating on the process, keeping it lively and quick, and making the boat move the way I wanted it to move. Although it took us eight strokes before our bow ball showed in front, the first time I was fully aware of what was going on around me was after about forty-five seconds. We were up. That felt good. We had the start we wanted. We always had a quick start, but this one was a good one: efficient, powerful, and quick. One box ticked, but nothing spectacular.

'The next marker, and the one where it really became external, is the one-minute marker where we called for a "stride". We looked to reach out and get hold of more length and power. The rate came down to 37 strokes a minute. Here we wanted our boat to move faster than the other five. I regarded finding the right cruising rhythm here as "my thing". One of the key parts of my race was the length and rhythm I gave the crew. In some ways, I left the start and finish to the power merchants around me. My job was to keep the boat moving sweetly. I allowed myself a little glance around. We were moving fast and in the way that I wanted to be moving. Steve commented later that after one minute he knew we'd win. Given the confidence that the race was in our hands, and that the boat was going the way we wanted it to, I remember thinking that things were going well. It was up to us. Yes we could win this. We expected to row away from the other crews. We had talked about moving ahead at one inch per stroke throughout the middle of the race.

'No one had blasted out. We could see all the opposition. We were able to do our bit. At 500 metres, we were 0.88 seconds ahead of the Australians in second place. We pushed, which took us a little bit further ahead. After 750 metres, I remember thinking we weren't as far ahead as I'd have liked, but I knew we were going to have a big push at 1000 metres. I thought about being efficient rather than panicking. At 1000 metres we were going to move away. We knew the Italians would push at around mid-race. We expected them to go with us. We thought that would be their plan. At 1000 metres, 0.46 seconds up on the Italians, we took the rate up to 38 strokes a minute. We moved up on the other crews, and, as expected, the Italians came with us. At 1250 metres, I was thinking the Italians were still there, still rating in the 40s. They were putting in a lot of energy into their rowing. *They can't keep that up*, I thought.

'Until that point, we weren't really aware of the Italians. In previous races they'd pushed from 750 metres gone to 1250 metres gone. We were keen to counter that, because it was also one of our strengths. In the final, not only did they play that card, but they kept it going for longer than we thought they were capable of. We weren't expecting the Italians to do what they did.

'By now, my body was screaming. I was feeling the burn, and had used up a lot of energy. I knew I had to put everything into the last 750 metres in order to win. We approached the third 500 metre section of the race, and thought once again that between 1250 metres gone and 500 metres to go, we'd move on. The boat still felt racy, but the Italians kept pushing, and came back a little bit in that third 500 metres. At 500 metres to go, they were 0.99 seconds down on us. At that point, we were going to lift and start rowing for the line. We took the rate up one pip. The Italians came up more. Matthew later said he was wishing the Italians would go away. To rate 39 to 40 strokes a minute is high for us, but the Italians were at 43, and still putting in the effort and energy.

'At this point, I'm starting to think, *Are they going to keep this up?* The last 500 metres were damage limitation. It was going to take them a superhuman effort to go through us. They'd already put that effort in. Between 500 metres to go and 250 to go, we increased the tempo. But when I reached for the extra gear, it wasn't there. I'd slotted into a rhythm and felt I could carry on, but when I asked my body for more, my body said, "No." The devils on each shoulder were pestering me and arguing among themselves. I remember thinking for the first time consciously not to make a mistake, a double-negative rather than a positive. I was thinking, *We will win, so long as we don't make a mistake*. But my body was fighting. My legs didn't want to move in one direction or another. The rest of the field was starting to close. I could tell Matthew was going for it. I was thinking, *Go on Matthew*. You could sense the field were on the move. We were fifth slowest in the last 500 metres. We had quickened, but the others had quickened more. I was still happy with the way the boat felt, but it was beginning to tire. The Italians were producing a race of which we hadn't thought they were capable. I remember being desperate for the red-buoys near to the Finish to come into sight. *They can't come quick enough*, I thought. Between 500 metres to go and 250 metres to go seemed an eternity. I was more confident with a minute gone than with one minute to go. Over the final 250 metres, we did 10 stroke step-ups. Every 10 strokes, we'd up the rate. At 100 metres to go, I allowed myself a glance, then put my head down and went for it. We were at 42, the Italians at 45. I was still confident. *Hang in there*, I thought, *and we've won*. I always thought we would win, but we had to give it our all. Had the Italians gone 0.5 of a second quicker in the early part of the race, perhaps they could have won. If you look at Steve and myself as we cross the line, there aren't many signs of another gear. If Matthew or James had it, personally I think they should have put that bit in. It was stubbornness that saw us through. Having had the overwhelming self-confidence before the race, it saw us through when we were seriously questioned in the last quarter.

'We crossed the line with a diminishing canvas lead over the Italians, having won by 0.38 seconds with the Australians third. It hurt. Everything caught up with me. A wave of pain and heat crashed over my body. Then I felt a we've-done-it feeling of elation begin building from the moment we crossed the line, crescendo and within five seconds overtake the pain. For sixteen years, I'd thought about what it would be like waiting for the rest of the world to catch up. I'd thought about it as a series of moments. But from the moment we crossed the line, it has never stopped. It was continuous. So much came together. Then we did something very unusual. We stopped rowing. Not really knowing what to do with myself, I punched the air and hit the water. After a lung-searing, gut-busting race like that, your muscles turn to jelly and you are barely in control of your movements. But what was this? While we gasped for breath, Matthew got up and began clambering over me. He should never have had the energy to do that. There were shades of the ergometer test back in March, when he pulled the second fastest ergo score of all time, then leapt up to help Steve. Having a sweaty Pinsent clambering over me wasn't the Olympic dream I'd envisaged. Matthew then tumbled into the water.

'One of the things that made it special was that 2000 people had travelled across the world to be there. The entire British swimming team were there too. A friend from Bedford swam out to us with a Union flag. Everyone was going ballistic, including us. Rowing past the grandstands and seeing the reaction of the crowds, I realised it wasn't just our gold medal, it was one that thousands of others shared with us. There was so much more to it than just the national anthem. In order of magnitude, this was a hundred times greater than I'd ever imagined. I'd dreamt of this moment for sixteen years, pushed through hard times and injury. When it finally happened, it was worth it ten times over. Still is. Nothing had prepared me for the way it felt, and the way it continues to feel.'

Once Pinsent had climbed back on board, the crew paddled over to the VIP side of the course and came ashore to speak to the assembled television cameras. Then they paddled across to the other side of the course and rowed past the kilometre of packed grandstands to acknowledge the crowds. Finally, they crossed the course once more to the medal pontoon, where the Princess Royal presented the medals, and where Juan Antonio Samaranch, President of the International Olympic Committee, stepped up and gave Redgrave a special gold Olympic pin.

Afterwards, Foster handed his medal to his mother, who burst into tears. 'When I'd gone through the lowest point of my back injury, she'd been my nurse as well as my mum. I always felt she'd understood what I'd gone through to do it.'

'Whenever he wins a medal he always puts it round my neck,' said Heather Foster. 'It's just one of the little things he does. And this time, I couldn't keep it. This is his medal and he ought to wear it. He should enjoy the glory of it for as long as he can, because it's truly wonderful.'

'I still can't help but smile when I think about that race,' says Foster. 'The feeling welling up and the pressure to get it out the evening before the final is the same ... I still feel it welling up.'

The Finish

That evening, the four never returned to their apartment in the Village, in order to avoid disrupting the eight, who were preparing to race the following day. The last thing the eight would have wanted was four staggering oarsmen bursting in with gold medals around their necks, grinning from ear to ear. It was a wise move. The next day, the eight caused the biggest surprise of the regatta by winning gold, beating the Australians by 0.8 seconds, the first Olympic victory by a British eight since 1912. Grobler's hopes of two gold medals were therefore borne out, but not in the way he had anticipated, since Coode and Searle just lost out on the medals by finishing fourth in their pairs final.

Later that day, as the oarsmen were packing up to make way for the canoeing regatta, the howling Penrith gale was already whipping up, forcing the organisers to postpone the erection of the canoeing course. One week later, the wind still howling, the canoeing finals were a farce of sinkings and capsizings.

Six days after the regatta had ended, Redgrave took Foster aside and very politely asked him to turn off his alarm clock, which had been set to ring at 4 a.m. Foster had never managed to return from partying until well after the alarm had already gone off.

On the flight home, all the British medallists flew Business Class; Redgrave and Pinsent were upgraded to First.

When the four reunited in November 2000 to row their boat from the Leander Club 400 metres upstream to the River and Rowing Museum, where it stands on display alongside the eight, the boat still had Redgrave's sugar taped inside. There it remained until a visitor filched it as a souvenir.

'You know,' said Foster to Redgrave some months later, 'even if we'd lost, it would still have been worth it.'

Acknowledgements

The authors would like to thank (in alphabetical order) James Cracknell, Chris Dodd, Bernie Ecclestone for coming up with the title, John Pilgrim-Morris, Maggie Netto for granting access to the Amateur Rowing Association's archive, Rachel Quarrell, Michael Rowe and Dan Topolski. Thanks also to Mr and Mrs Brian Foster, and Henrietta Royle, for their time in reading and commenting on the typescript. They would also like to thank David Luxton and Richard Milner of Orion for their patience. Rory Ross would in particular like to apologise to all the other editors whom he has annoyed while writing this book – they know who they are.

Bibliography

The main sources for this book are the reminiscences and diaries of Tim Foster, and the many volumes of race reports, crew diaries and interviews with crew members that were published during the lifespan of the Sydney coxless four and which may be located in the archive at the Amateur Rowing Association's headquarters at Hammersmith and in the library of the River and Rowing Museum, Mill Meadows, Henley-on-Thames, Oxfordshire RG9 1BF.

Halberstam, David, *The Amateurs*, Fawcett Columbine, New York, 1985.
Redgrave, Steve, with Nick Townsend, *A Golden Age*, BBC Worldwide Limited, 2000.
Regatta magazine, passim.
Yallop, Richard, *Oarsome*, Ironbark, Pan Macmillan Australia, 1998.

Index

8, 40; physical ability, 34; attitude to rowing, 35, 115–16; early career, 35–8; physique, 36; maverick reputation, 38, 40; perfectionism, 40; team launch, 42–4; poor eyesight, 47; diet, 51–2, 85, 149–50; domestic life, 52–3; and media, 54–6, 89; recognised by public, 57; coaching, 58–9, 128–9, 133; stylistic faults, 58; position in boat, 59; Sports Aid funding, 63; sponsorship, 64–5; friendly attitude to opponents, 68; first World Championship win, 71; hair dyeing, 81, 86; social life, 85–6, 88, 119, 155, 192; paired with Martin Cross, 86; accident to hand, 86–90, 119; rejoins team, 91–2; technique, 104, 117; back problem, 106–12, 113–14, 152, 182–4; singing, 116–17; return to training, 118–21; in British eight, 122–4, 127–30; struggle for Olympics four place, 125–7, 131–8; room-mate with Coode, 132, 151; good relations with Coode, 133, 151–2; boat-moving abilities, 133; injures hand, 134; pairs trial and rift in team, 142–8; back in four, 146–8; sense of humour, 156; football excursion to Belgium, 159–61; weight, 165, 173; describes race, 186–90; gives medals to mother, 190–1
French language, 30

Gainsville, 19
Gates, Bill, 26
gearing, 10
Germans, 67
Ginn, Drew, 92
Gladiators, 26
Gold Coast, 113, 131–2
golf contest, 157–8
Grandstand, 7
Great Ouse, 35

Green, Nick, 92
Grobler, Jürgen: personality, 1–2; pre-race talk, 2–3; pre-race preparations, 9–10; selects team, 28, 31, 33–4, 36–40; training, 46–7, 49–50, 57–62, 75–6, 101, 131; misses flight, 72; cycling training, 75, 113; separation of private life from rowing, 80, 82, 83–4, 153; enthusiasm for training camps, 80–1; view of alcohol, 85; and Foster's accident, 89–91; early starts, 119; and Foster's return, 121–3; Olympics selection, 125–7, 133, 135–8, 145–8; and Martin McElroy, 128; congratulates Foster, 130; has words with Redgrave, 141; paternal instincts, 147; and diet, 149; announces Olympic selections, 150–2; responsibility for Lucerne defeat, 165; dress, 171–2; achieves hope of two gold medals, 191
Grubor, Luka, 86–7, 151; takes Foster's place, 89, 117, 121–2
Grünau Regatta, 60
Guardian, 29
Gunn, Steve, 20

Hamilton, Richard, 33
Hampton Grammar School, 19, 20, 34, 36
Hanson, Bo, 163
Harpenden Hospital, 108–9
Hazewinkel, 40, 91, 120–1
Head of the River race, 57, 106, 134
Henley-on-Thames, 27, 32, 41, 44–6, 54, 90, 101, 106, 131, 159, 160; Bridge, 42, 44, 45; Rowing and River Museum, 4, 167, 192
Henley Reach, 45, 47, 57
Henley Royal Regatta, 29, 32, 44, 45, 124, 156, 162–3, 165, 166; Stewards' Challenge Cup, 3, 68–9, 92–4